Much mo

calamari

Octavia the Octopus

About the Author

Octavia the Octopus was born in the Mediterranean Sea just off the shores of Southern Spain. She was one of two hundred and fifty thousand siblings who were released as eggs into the plankton by their mother. During the time she was floating in the sea she travelled extensively, visiting waters off the Balearic Islands, Algeria and Morocco. This was a formative experience for her and one which gave her an international perspective of the world.

At the age of fifty days Octavia settled down to a benthic existence in a small submerged rock crevice close to Gibraltar. There she divided her time between catching and eating crabs and mussels, keeping her lair clean by dumping their empty shells outside and exploring the seabed. After several months she moved to another larger fissure, and finally to a purpose-built terra-cotta cylinder. She attributes her itinerant lifestyle to the lack of parental role models and early separation from her siblings, the majority of whom are thought to have been eaten by predatory fish.

Octavia's final choice of residence proved to be an octopus pot and she quickly found herself hauled on board a Spanish fishing boat from the port of Algeciras. In company with several dozen other octopuses, when the ship docked she was taken to the nearby fish market where, for reasons that were never explained to her, she was selected by an aquarium keeper from the local sea-life centre. Her companions, she believes, all pursued short careers in the catering trade.

Life changed dramatically for Octavia at the sea life centre. With food supplied to her daily she was freed from the need to go hunting, so she devoted her daytime to the observation and recording of human behaviour through the sides of her tank. Intrigued by this species which had been previously unknown to her, after closing time at the aquarium she embarked on a study of its history. By comparing her knowledge of molluscan history with the human perspective of events, it soon became apparent that they had been interpreted very differently. The role of molluscs in shaping the human world had received the barest minimum of recognition. Through this book she sets out to rectify the situation and to prove to human readers that molluscs are much more than calamari.

Acknowledgments

Octavia wishes to acknowledge the contributions made by Dr Paul Sharpe to the publication of this book.

Contents

1

Of Crustaceous and Testaceous Fishes

As a species humans are a self-centred lot when it comes to the relating of events. They tell of their heroic figures of the past, the battles they fought, the dynasties they founded and the great cities, civilisations and inventions they created as if they did it all on their own. With a few exceptions they always put themselves centre-stage in the drama. Rarely do they recognise the invaluable contribution to their successes made by animals, and then only really in a supporting role. Genghis Khan is remembered for the way in which his Mongol tribesmen swept across huge areas of Europe and Asia, but they would not have achieved such dramatic conquests without the horses on which they rode. Deprived of his elephants to create panic and confusion in the ranks of the Roman army, Hannibal could well have been on the losing side in the battle of Cannae. Lawrence of Arabia might easily have remained an unknown figure had it not been for the camels on which his Arab troops were dependent, and the European colonisation of Southern Africa might have taken a very different turn without the oxen to draw the carts of the early settlers.

Such examples show that human history undoubtedly has been shaped by animals, but in all these cases, the animals involved were, like humans themselves, mammals. It is perhaps unsurprising, therefore, that they should have developed a close relationship with them and grudgingly afforded them a few lines in print. How different it is when it comes to other animal groups, especially those, like mine, without fur or even a backbone. Now I will put that down to their ignorance of the contribution that invertebrates, including us molluscs, have made, rather than to any actual prejudice. Why should that ignorance have arisen? Whilst I cannot answer for the other phyla, in part the fault lies with us, for we are naturally self-effacing as well as being something of a strange and varied bunch of animals altogether.

Back in the eighteenth century Oliver Goldsmith wrote about us in his book '*A History of the Earth and Animated Nature*'. The science of natural classification was still in its infancy and he placed us in a group of animals called "shellfish", which at first sight is not a bad description as many of us do indeed live inside shells. Unfortunately he ignored the fact that tortoises and turtles have leathery rather than calcareous shells, an internal skeleton, and their even more obvious possession of legs and a head, and included them in the same group. Would humans classify themselves as close relatives of ostriches on the grounds that they also run around on two legs? He then compounded his error by assigning the cuttlefish - a close relative of mine - into a completely different group along with starfish on the basis that they both have arms.

To some extent amends were made when the "shellfish" were then sub-divided, with the crabs, lobsters, tortoises and turtles being separated out as "crustaceous fish", whilst we molluscs were designated as "testaceous fish". Here again, however, Oliver Goldsmith made another serious mistake. With us he included barnacles, since they too have shells which are also calcareous and superficially similar to ours. Had he really not considered that they had tiny,

2

jointed legs that protruded from their shells when they were immersed in water? It took the genius of Charles Darwin, nearly one hundred years later, to realise they were in fact crustaceans, and therefore related to crabs and lobsters and not to us at all. So with all this confusion, perhaps Oliver Goldsmith should have stuck to what most humans remember him for today, as an author and playwright.

Thankfully modern day biologists have a much better understanding of our true relationships with other animals and they put all molluscs into the Phylum Mollusca. This, in turn, is divided into six classes. Three of them do not have many members and have not moved on with the times, surviving a little like living fossils. The other three though have something in the order of eighty thousand living species between them and, after the Phylum Arthropoda, belong to the most abundant phylum of invertebrates. It is members of these classes who have so influenced human society, and although you will almost certainly have encountered them, let me briefly remind you who they are.

Snails and their slimy naked relatives, slugs, are in the largest class numerically, called the Gastropoda. Living on land, under the sea and in fresh water, they typically move by gliding over the ground on a thick, muscular foot. Indeed their manner of locomotion gives a clue to their name, being derived from the Latin words *gaster,* meaning stomach, and *pous,* meaning foot. As I will show in the following chapters, these seemingly insignificant animals have been responsible for the downfall of cities and contributed to the splendour of ancient Rome, whilst without them the trans-Atlantic slave trade might never have taken place.

The second main class is the Bivalvia and no one would have difficulty in recognising its members. They are all found in water, both sea and fresh, and have two hinged shells or valves, hence their name. Many live quite secretive lives, buried in sand or mud, and are only noticed when they are dead and their empty shells are washed onto the shore. Yet without their actions in life, the cathedral city of Santiago de Compostela would not exist and England could have become a Spanish colony.

Which brings me to the class to which I belong. As an octopus, I am in the Cephalopoda along with the squids and cuttlefish. We are a little bit different from each other in that we octopuses have eight arms whereas they have ten, but that is no handicap to me and in most other ways we are similar. The majority of us have dispensed with our shells to enable us to swim more easily, and with our large eyes, a beaked mouth and arms to help us capture our prey, I can quite understand why humans did not know how to classify us for so long.

Apart from our appearance being so dissimilar from the other members of the Mollusca, the feature that really sets us apart is our intelligence. Without wishing to be too unkind to them, the bivalves and the gastropods barely have enough nerve cells to make a nervous system, let alone sufficient to cluster together to form a brain. Ours brains are well developed though and so, being blessed with one, I intend to use it, and through this book show that without the molluscs – all of them and not just the Cephalopoda – human history, society and culture would have been very different from what they are today.

2

A copper-bottomed guarantee

Far from their home port and faced with strong winds and angry seas, the men on board the Spanish galleon *El Gran Grifon* must have viewed the rugged coastline of Fair Isle with more than a little apprehension. The flagship of the Spanish Armada's supply squadron, it mounted thirty eight guns and was carrying over two hundred soldiers in addition to the crew. Since mid-July, when Sir Francis Drake had attacked it in his ship *Revenge*, it had sailed out of the English Channel, into the North Sea, and far beyond the Scottish mainland. Now it was 27th September 1588 and the crew were anxious to make repairs in a safe haven before setting out into the Atlantic Ocean for the long run back to Spain.

The source of their anxiety was that *El Gran Grifon* was leaking. In part this was due to the damage that had been inflicted on it by English cannon balls, but a small mollusc called *Teredo navalis* may well have started the rot, quite literally, several years earlier. Let me explain.

Better known as a shipworm – and here the humans show their ignorance, for these creatures are bivalve molluscs, not worms – *Teredo navalis* lives in seawater and loves to eat wood. Any type of wood submerged in sea water will do, and a ship's wooden hull is a veritable banquet for them. Within a short time a good colony can turn a watertight hull into one that is honey-combed with tunnels, waterlogged, crumbling away and leaking.

A shipworm starts off life as a microscopic planktonic larva drifting in the sea, until it locates its future home by detecting the wood chemically. Once settled on the surface of the wood, it metamorphoses and begins its lifetime's work of burrowing. As a bivalve mollusc, *Teredo* has a pair of shells, like cockles and mussels do, but *Teredo* has modified its shells to act like drill bits with abrasive serrations on the front edge. By rasping through the timber it penetrates ever deeper, enlarging the diameter of the tunnel as it grows. To use its shells so effectively they have been reduced in size and are no longer large enough to enclose the animal's soft body, so it secretes a smooth calcareous lining to its tube. Safe inside from predators, it draws clean oxygenated water over its gills using a pair of long, hollow, fleshy tubes called siphons that poke out from the open end. A fully grown shipworm's greatly elongated body can easily grow to twenty centimetres in length, and with a diameter of only centimetre or so, it is understandable that *Teredo* was not recognised as being a mollusc until 1733.

Like most bivalves, it can also use its gills to filter food particles from the water, but *Teredo* has little need to do so. Courtesy of symbiotic bacteria living in its gut, it is able to get its energy from the cellulose in the wood in which it lives, passing any undigested material, resembling sawdust, out of the open end of the burrow. The open end can also be blocked off as the tips of the siphons carry a pair of calcareous plates; valuable assets when humans try to get rid of them.

King Philip II of Spain began assembling his invasion fleet several years before it embarked for England; years in which the shipworms started their feasting on his ships' hulls. By the time they set sail, many of his vessels were in a poor state of repair, although history usually credits the superior seamanship of the English sailors in bringing about the Armada's defeat. Certainly seamanship played its part, with the English ships keeping to windward of the Spanish fleet. Heeled over by the wind, this would have exposed their hulls below the waterline to the English cannon balls – hulls already weakened by *Teredo*.

Fire-ships sent into the Armada when it lay at anchor in the Calais Roads caused it to scatter, and on 29th July a number of Spanish ships were sunk or driven onto the sandbanks off Gravelines. This was the last serious engagement between the two fleets and, unable to return homeward through the English Channel, the ragged Armada sailed onwards through the North Sea. Of the one hundred and thirty vessels that set out from Spain, only half of them returned. Fifty one of those which failed were wrecked, and one of those was *El Gran Grifon*. She foundered on the rocks of Stomshellier, leaving fifty men dead on Fair Isle. Altogether over thirteen thousand soldiers were lost and two thousand held prisoner. The Armada's defeat had been emphatic.

With the threat of invasion averted, England rejoiced and the English commanders, Lord Howard of Effingham, Sir Francis Drake and Sir John Hawkins, became national heroes, their deeds celebrated in words, engravings and paintings. That nature also played a part in the Armada's defeat was recognised soon after the victory had become clear. A commemorative medal was struck and carried the inscription "*Afflavit Deau et dissipantur*" – "God blew and they were scattered". Undoubtedly the wind did favour the English in the running battle along the Channel, and the gales which followed broke the Armada as a fighting unit.

Now whilst I am not disputing that God deserved due credit, as far as I am aware, no similar medal of recognition of the part played by *Teredo navalis* has ever been produced. What an oversight that has been.

And on the subject of oversights, the outcome of Philip II's Armada might have been a very different one had he and his admirals learned from another one which sailed during his father's reign.

When, on Wednesday 10th September 1522, the weather beaten and shipworm riddled ship *Victoria* tied up alongside the quay of the Guadalquivir River in Seville, for its decimated and scurvy ridden crew it marked the welcome end of an epic voyage which had seen them become the first Europeans to circumnavigate the world. *Victoria* had been one of five ships which formed the Armada de Molucca, and which had set out from that port some three years previously on a quest to find a new route to the fabled Spice Islands. In that the expedition had achieved its aim, but had it not been for shipworm it could have made its financial backers immensely rich as well.

The expedition had been led by a Portuguese mariner, Fernao de Magalhaes who, having failed to persuade his own king to sponsor such a venture, moved to Spain, where he became known as Fernando de Magallanes. At that time Portugal and Spain were rival powers for opening up and exploiting the resources of the New World. This ill-defined part of the world referred to anywhere beyond Europe and across the Ocean Sea, as the Atlantic Ocean was then called. As a consequence of their rivalry, in 1494 Pope Alexander VI issued a Papal Bull which effectively divided the world into two halves. Extending from pole to pole, this demarcation line ran through the Atlantic Ocean, with Spain being granted exclusive rights to those parts of the world that lay to the west of the line, whilst those to the east were Portuguese. What had appeared to be a simple solution to the problem of competition between the two countries however proved to be no such thing, for with no accurate means of establishing a vessel's longitude, the question of in which hemisphere the Spice Islands lay was a matter of conjecture. One matter though was certain. If Spain was to have a sea-route to them, it would have to be found by sailing west around South America rather than by an easterly one through Portuguese waters. It was Fernando de Magallanes, who persuaded King Charles I of Spain that he was the man who could do it.

From the outset the Armada de Molucca was beset by misfortune, and even before it had left the Atlantic, its smallest ship was wrecked and its largest one slipped away and set sail back to Spain. Undeterred by these setbacks, Magellan pressed on and succeeded in finding the channel that separates the mainland of South America from the island of Tierra del Fuego, and which today bears his name. His three remaining ships then headed off into the vastness of the Pacific, eventually reaching the island of Mactan in the Philippines, and here it was that Magellan was killed in a battle with the forces of the local king, Lapu-Lapu. Tragic as it had been, in the minds of the remaining captains, there was no question of turning back, but the Spice Islands that they may have imagined lay just a short way ahead, took them over another six months to reach.

On 8th November 1521, the Armada de Molucca finally arrived at the islands after which it had been named, and entered the harbour of one of the principal ones, Tidore. Trading for cloves began immediately, and by mid-December the ships' holds, and every other conceivable space, were crammed with the fragrant scented buds and the ships made ready to sail.

Even before she had left the harbour though, disaster struck the Armada's flagship, *Trinidad*. On board were one thousand quintals, or five tons, of cloves, but all were in danger of being lost as she began to leak and to take in large volumes of water. The cause of the leak could not be explained by witnesses to the catastrophe, but as the expedition's chronicler Antonio Pigafetta wrote: "*We found that water was rushing in as through a pipe, but we were unable to find where it was coming in.*" In my opinion, the many months spent at sea had allowed the shipworm to do their worst, and the hull was in a generally unseaworthy condition. Why do I feel confident in saying this?

Five days after the death of Ferdinand Magellan, whilst the Armada threaded its way between shoals and uncharted islands of the Philippines, the captain of the *Concepcion*, a ship of similar size to *Victoria*, reported that her hull was riddled with shipworm. Eighteen months at sea had allowed the mollusc population to grow to epidemic proportions. The options facing the expedition were severely limited, for there were insufficient crewmen left to man the pumps, or to carry out the extensive repairs that would have been necessary, whilst to simply abandon it would risk letting it fall into the hands of the Portuguese. Instead the rotting ship was set ablaze, leaving the expedition comprising merely two ships, *Victoria* and *Trinidad*.

After three months of repairs at Tidore, *Trinidad* finally left the port with her precious cargo of cloves, only to return there seven months later after wandering aimlessly through the Pacific. With only a handful of survivors, the captain surrendered his ship to the Portuguese who by then were back in control of the island. Shortly afterwards, a violent storm struck the island and *Trinidad* was smashed to pieces and the cloves went with her to the bottom of the sea.

As the sole survivor of the Armada de Molucca, *Victoria* began her homeward journey across the Indian Ocean and around the Cape of Good Hope. Almost certainly she also suffered from the ravages of *Teredo* because as she passed familiar landmarks along the coast of North Africa, her hull began to let in water, and her severely depleted and malnourished crew were forced to man the pumps continuously just to keep her afloat. Only when the ship tied up in Seville could they stop.

For the expedition's financial backers, the 524 quintals (52,400lbs) of cloves in *Victoria's* hold was sufficiently valuable to recoup their investment, but how much more would their profit have been if *Trinidad* and *Concepcion* had remained seaworthy and returned with her?

The shipworm's hunger for wooden ships did not stop with Magellan's expedition or Philip II's Armada. Little wonder therefore, that some two hundred years later, and with countless other *Teredo*-riddled ships foundering, Linnaeus, the founder of the modern biological classification system, gave them their original scientific name of *Calamitas navium*.

I rather prefer this name, with its descriptive implications, to the modern one but I doubt that the sailors of the *Cinque Ports* would have agreed with me back in 1709. In that year their vessel, riddled with shipworm, foundered off the Pacific coast of present day Colombia, with only a handful of the crew, including the captain, surviving. The shipworms' actions marked the end of the voyage for the *Cinque Ports*, but five years earlier they had triggered a chain of events which resulted in the writing of, what many literary critics regard as, the first English novel.

At that time, Captain Stradling, the commander of the *Cinque Ports*, was being warned that his vessel was unseaworthy by one of his own seamen. There may have been more to the discussion than just the state of repair of the ship, but the result of their meeting was that Captain Stradling ignored the advice and the seaman asked to be put ashore on a deserted island many miles from normal sea routes. As another mariner of the time, Captain Woodes Rogers later wrote on being told of the incident by the marooned seaman himself:

> *'The reason of his being left here was a difference betwixt him and his captain; which, together with the ships being leaky, made him willing rather to stay here...'*

Had the abandoned man been anything other than extremely resourceful, it is unlikely that he would have survived those next five years of isolation. He did, however, and it was Captain Woodes Rogers who then found him. Captain Woodes Rogers was not on a rescue mission but was sailing past that deserted island by chance whilst in search of Spanish treasure ships. On Rogers' return to England, he wrote a book in which he gave an account of his capture of a Spanish ship, his circumnavigation of the globe, and the rescue of a goat-skin clad mariner from that deserted island of Juan Fernandez. His book, *'A Cruising Voyage Round the World'*, was published in 1712, with a second edition in 1718, and in it he gives a vivid account of the marooned man's existence.

In 1719, Daniel Defoe published *'The Life and Strange Surprizing Adventures of Robinson Crusoe, of York, Mariner: Who lived Eight and Twenty Years, all alone in an un-inhabited Island on the Coast of America, near the Mouth of the Great River of Oroonoque; Having been cast on Shore by Shipwreck, wherein all the Men perished but himself. With An Account how he was at last as strangely deliver'd by Pirates.'* 'Robinson Crusoe' proved to be a much more catchy and memorable title. His central character bears so many similarities to the real life castaway on Jean Fernandez Island, a man called Alexander Selkirk, that Woodes Rogers' book was almost certainly its inspiration. Selkirk had no Man Friday or a pet goat, and never encountered cannibals, but where would the English novel be without the actions of *Teredo navalis*?

Since antiquity, every seafaring nation has known about the ravages of shipworm and all sought to prevent damage to their ships by them. The oldest method was simply to haul the ship onto dry land. There its bottom could be scraped clear of the fouling of seaweed and barnacles, and the timbers allowed to dry out. As they did so, the shipworms would eventually die, but with water trapped inside the tunnels by the calcareous plates plugging the open end, this could take some time. Their tunnels, however, would remain and refill with water when the ship was refloated, and the timbers once again open to attack by *Teredo*. It would be only a matter of time before the vessel was fit only for firewood.

Greek and Roman galleys were small enough to be pushed up the beach on rollers, but as ships became larger, so the technique of careening was developed. Taken to a quiet backwater, ballast and most of the rigging was removed. The lightened ship would then float well out of the water and would be beached at high tide. Using ropes attached to sturdy positions on the shore and windlasses on the ship, the vessel would gradually be tilted over to rest on one side. The exposed part of the hull could then be cleaned, the ship re-floated and the other side of the hull dealt with in a similar manner. This technique was most effective in tropical climates where the hot sun would speed up the process, but was backbreaking work. Taking a ship into a river was another old solution, for *Teredo* cannot tolerate living in fresh water. It would take several days however before the river water could penetrate the tunnels, so like being dragged out of the sea, the ships would have been out of use for some time and the timbers still honeycombed. A more technological solution was required, and prevention of infestation was even better than cure.

Just about anything that could be coated onto a ship's hull has been tried to prevent attack by shipworm. Tar, pitch, fish-oil and tallow have all been smeared on, but none lasted long in the water, so frequent scraping and recoating was still necessary. Sheathing the underside of the ship in lead was also used with good effect, albeit with two serious disadvantages. Adding weight to the vessel is the obvious one, as the people whose job it was to fix the metal to the wood must have realised. Thin sheets were all that was needed, but even ones as thin as only one millimetre would have given additional weight of over six kilogrammes per square metre. Fixing the sheets would also have required iron nails, and these created the second drawback. Lead is lower on the electrochemical scale than iron, so when the two are next to each other in seawater, the iron nails act as sacrificial anodes. In other words, the iron reacts more quickly than the lead with the seawater, resulting in the iron nails breaking down. Any iron nails in the vicinity of the lead would have been affected. Not only would the lead plates have been likely to fall off, but even the nails which held the ship's hull together would have been imperilled.

Humans then tried other metals with which to sheath their ships, and copper, at about two thirds of the density of lead, was found to be an effective, albeit more expensive, way of protecting them. The first record of this was in 1761 when the British Royal Navy clad the hull of HMS *Alarm* with copper. After a two year cruise, the Admiralty were informed "*that so long as copper plates can be kept upon the bottom, the planks will be thereby entirely secured from the effects of the worm.*"

Perhaps with this in mind, when Captain James Cook set off on his five year voyage of discovery in 1766 his ship, HMS *Endeavour*, was well protected by this new technique. Warm, tropical waters favour the growth of shipworm, and much of his time was spent in cruising the waters of the South Pacific Ocean. His highly successful expedition stopped off in South America, mapped the coastline of New Zealand and then sailed along the unexplored East coast of Australia. Landfall was first made there at a place he named Botany Bay as a consequence of the profusion of new plants encountered there. It must have been a paradise for the young botanist on the expedition, Joseph Banks.

Banks' reputation was made by the discoveries that he made whilst with Cook. Each time the *Endeavour* dropped anchor, he went ashore collecting vast numbers of plants that were new to science, including *Bougainvillea* and *Gardenia.* From Botany Bay alone he collected over eight hundred species. Following his return to England he became prominent in the founding of the colony of New South Wales and an advisor in the establishment of the Royal Botanic Gardens at Kew.

Copper sheathing, however, proved no match for the jagged coral of the Great Barrier Reef and the ship was holed, yet its protected timbers remained sufficiently strong that it could be beached, repaired and eventually sailed home to England. Had HMS *Endeavour* succumbed to the ravages of *Teredo*, James Cook might have remained an obscure mariner, the presence of Botany Bay remained unknown to the British, the penal colony not set up there, and the subsequent colonisation of Australia and New Zealand been carried out by other nations.

If the defeat of the Spanish Armada was due in part to their vessels being infested with shipworm, then at the Battle of Trafalgar in 1805, Admiral Nelson could have been confident that his ships were free from them. Following the trials on HMS *Alarm*, it became commonplace to clad ships of the Royal Navy with copper, and in 1780 the hull below the waterline of his flagship HMS *Victory* was sheathed with 3,923 such sheets. French and Spanish cannon balls may have destroyed the rigging and ripped through the wooden walls of his fleet, but beneath the waves, his vessel was 'sound'; a maritime insurance term indicating that a ship had suffered no damage on its voyage.

Copper sheathing was also used on merchant ships, and vessels treated in this way, being more seaworthy, were given preferential rates by insurance companies. Thus, a 'copper bottom guarantee' gave a better level of assurance that it would survive its voyage than one without, and that it would return 'safe and sound'. The 'safe' in this phrase referring to none of the crew being lost or injured.

Since the Middle Ages, farmers in what is now the Netherlands reclaimed marshes and fenland to create fertile polders. To prevent the incursion of the drained land by the sea, the polders were protected by embankments of earth, but as this would quickly be washed away, the seaward sides were then faced with timber. In 1730, the Dutch were recording a huge infestation of 'pileworms' in the wood of the dike system of Friesland, and careful study by the Dutch zoologist, Gotfren Snellius, revealed it was not worms that were doing the damage, but molluscs. They were none other than *Teredo* in another setting.

With kilometres of dikes, the shipworms would have been as happy as human children gazing on rows of sweet jars in a confectioner's shop, and they munched into the wood with gusto. By 1731, *Teredo* had destroyed fifty kilometres of piling and damaged another twenty. A storm in that year then breached the weakened defences and large parts of the area were flooded.

After the disaster, the Dutch tried various methods of protecting their dikes. Coating the wood with solutions containing arsenic might have had some benefit but with unknown environmental consequences. Iron plates fixed on the surface of the piles could have given temporary protection until they rusted away, and whilst tropical hardwoods took longer to be eaten away than temperate woods, eventually they too succumbed. In the end only impenetrable and inedible stone revetments proved a match for *Teredo*.

With the area's heavy dependence on agriculture, the effects of the 1731 flooding was catastrophic. Farm labourers were forced off the land and into unemployment, whilst to pay for the stone, most of which had to be imported at great cost, additional taxes had to be raised. For a while the whole Dutch economy was imperilled as a consequence of shipworm. Their new sea defences held however, and never again did *Teredo* have the opportunity to cause so much damage.

Leastwise in the Netherlands, but humans can be slow learners. Two hundred years later, and thousands of miles away on the shores of the Pacific, they were still feasting on wooden structures and doing huge damage to them.

Between 1919 and 1921, in San Francisco Bay, piers, wharves and ferry slips collapsed as a consequence of their actions, resulting in repairs costing an estimated $900 million. Reconstruction was in steel and cement, materials which, in combination with an imitation of *Teredo*'s own burrowing technique, led to the construction of one of the world's greatest feats of civil engineering.

On 6th May 1994, after eight thousand years of separation, Great Britain was once again joined to mainland Europe, albeit through a tunnel beneath the waters of the English Channel. The Queen and France's President Mitterand cut red, white and blue ribbons to ceremonially open the route which, with a length of fifty kilometres, became the longest international tunnel and the longest underwater tunnel in the world.

It all began back in the early nineteenth century when Marc Brunel, the father of Isambard Kingdom Brunel, was observing a group of *Teredo* eating through wood in a tank of sea water at Chatham Dockyard. Brunel, a French naval engineer and fugitive from the French Revolution, was impressed by the manner in which they used their shells like drill bits to bore into the wood, and then lined their burrow with a smooth coating of calcium as they progressed. This gave him the idea to create a tunnelling shield in which a miner could work, cutting into the rock in front of him without the danger of collapse. As it drove forwards, so the tunnel behind was lined with brick.

With this ingenious system, Brunel undertook construction of the world's first tunnel beneath a navigable waterway, the river Thames. Started at Rotherhithe in 1825 and with a length of a little under four hundred metres, progress was tediously slow. It took eighteen years for the tunnellers to reach the opposite side at Wapping, giving an average speed of about sixty millimetres a day; a rate that would not disgrace a shipworm. On its completion, at first it was used by pedestrians only, but it also became a major tourist attraction for people visiting London. From 1865, thanks to the generous headroom inside that Brunel had created, it then became a railway tunnel and some years later it was incorporated into the London Underground system. Today, almost 150 years after its completion, it is still used by trains of London Overground.

Following on from Marc Brunel's pioneering work, several other tunnels using refinements of his system were built in Britain. Mechanical drill heads replaced men with picks and shovels to cut through the rock, and steel and concrete made faster and stronger linings than brick, but the basic technique remained the same. From 1988, at an average rate of progress of seven thousand metres a year, the Channel Tunnel's boring machines ate through the chalk beneath the sea bed to physically re-unite England with France two years later. Today trains convey their passengers and freight between the two countries, with those from England emerging near Calais; fittingly near to where *Teredo navali*s played such an important part in the destruction of the Spanish Armada.

3

"...poverty and oysters always seems to go together."

Marinated raw with vinegar or lime juice and served with chopped chilli pepper and onions, *Teredo* is considered to be a delicacy in some parts of the Pacific, but being quite small and difficult to get at, they have never formed a significant part of the diet of humans in that region. On a global scale, how to cook other molluscs such as clams, or to include them in paella, often features in their recipe books, and there can hardly be a seaside town anywhere in the world without its seafood restaurant. As a food that has sustained them over millennia though, humans have written remarkably little about us in their history books.

It was appropriately in France, that country renowned for its love of eating snails, where early man is known to have first consumed molluscs. At a site called Terra Amata on the Mediterranean coast some 300,000 years ago, hominids, those early ancestors of present day humans, *Homo sapiens,* feasted on shellfish and left the discarded shells behind as evidence. Similar prehistoric middens have been unearthed from around the world, seemingly wherever Neanderthal man or *Homo sapiens* settled by the sea. Neanderthal man, however, was doomed for extinction, and by about 30,000 years ago he had disappeared. *Homo sapiens* though continued to flourish, but modern humans have never come up with a wholly satisfactory explanation about the demise of their nearest relatives. Genocide and interbreeding have both been suggested, but they have consistently overlooked the part played by us molluscs.

Marine and terrestrial proteins have slightly different chemical compositions, and after they have been digested and rebuilt into human bones, this difference can be detected. Analysis of ancient bones can therefore show what early man had been eating. Neanderthals, it seems, preferred to get their protein from land living mammals whereas *Homo sapiens* had a wider diet including much more shellfish. So when wild game became scarce, this would have affected *Homo sapiens* much less than the Neanderthals, perhaps to the extent that they were starved out of existence.

Even then life was still not easy for *Homo sapiens*, and after surviving the rigours of the Ice Age, so he then was faced by rising sea levels as the glaciers and ice caps melted. The associated climate change affected his food supply and he might well have gone the same way as the Neanderthals without us to sustain him. Rising sea levels were of no concern and we were abundant, and were consumed in ever increasing numbers.

And what a wonderful food we were too. It makes me wonder why humans bothered to go hunting those wild and dangerous beasts that roamed the land. We live buried in sand or mud, or cling to rocks, but are always easy to find. Even children and old people, who would have been useless in a hunt, could gather us. It takes no tools, expertise or great strength to collect us and, as we do not migrate, we are there all the year around. Yet despite these obvious advantages, humans largely shunned us and set about the long, often dangerous and sometimes fatal process of domestication of animals instead. Only in unusual situations or in times of famine did they turn back to us, as Oliver Goldsmith wrote of the eighteenth century's "... *poorer inhabitants of several of the Western Isles of Scotland*" for whom:

> *"Periwinkles and limpets, which so profusely stud the rocks of their shores, are their daily fare, and on which they are sometimes reduced to the necessity of altogether subsisting".*

With the almost indifferent attitude towards human suffering prevalent at the time, he commented further on the situation on the Isle of Skye where:

> *"...we are told that there is almost usually a degree of famine, when the poor are left to Providence's care, and prowl, like other animals, along the shore, to pick up limpets and other shell-fish..."*

Centuries earlier though, the Romans regarded shellfish not as subsistence fare, but as luxury items. They loved seafood, and as they conquered new territories, including Britain, so they took their appetite for shellfish with them. Even those living far inland were not forgotten. Packed into ice, whelks, cockles, mussels and limpets were transported to towns and villages across the colony, and even the soldiers serving on Hadrian's Wall were not deprived. And of all the molluscs that ended up on the Romans' tables, none were more highly prized and had a greater influence in shaping British history than oysters. Called "ostrea" in Latin, they retain that link in their scientific name of *Ostrea edulis*, the edible oyster.

In AD 43, the Romans invaded Britain and quickly established their first colony in Colchester, not I believe as humans usually record, for strategic purposes, but because of the oysters that they found there. So good were they that they were even transported as far as Rome; an export trade which brought little benefit to the native inhabitants of the region. Outraged by the perceived theft of their oysters, under the leadership of Boudicca, the Icini and other tribes of Southern Britain revolted, and in AD 61 razed Colchester to the ground. Although it was subsequently rebuilt and became a major centre throughout the Roman occupation, it never regained its former status, and now is a market town with a Roman wall and a castle built over the sub-structure of the Temple of Claudius. Instead fate dictated that a formerly less significant settlement, Londinium, became pre-eminent and, as London, went on to become the centre of an empire that eclipsed that of the Romans. Maybe it is as a mark of respect to the many oysters which almost certainly perished and were cooked in the flames that at the annual Colchester oyster festival, they are eaten raw.

For much of the eighteenth century, Britain was engaged in wars with France and needed to obtain money to finance them. Taxes were raised and so, in turn, people had to find a way of increasing their income. For the oystermen of the east coast of England the answer was to step up exports, and in the Dutch they found a ready market. The North Sea could be a dangerous stretch of water to cross in their oyster smacks, which were designed more for coastal waters, but the rewards were worth the risk and men from such ports as Faversham in Kent grew rich. On a good trip, a boatload of oysters could fetch up to £350 – a small fortune in those days.

It would quickly have become apparent to the oystermen that to return home in an empty vessel was uneconomic when a cargo could be carried, and with high taxes on luxury items such as tea, tobacco, lace, brandy and rum, it must have seemed prudent, albeit illegal, to put some of these sought after goods on board. With customs' men waiting in the ports, unloading their illicit cargo there would have risked confiscation and imprisonment, so quiet creeks and backwaters, of which the region has an abundance, were preferred. The oystermen, with their intimate knowledge of the coastline and shallow draughted vessels, found secluded moorings where their contraband could be unloaded and stored until it could be moved on. The local inhabitants were generally sympathetic to these honest fishermen but who were now considered to be smugglers in the eyes of the law, so only those who saw tax evasion as a crime would speak out against them. One such person was Daniel Defoe, who wrote in his book, '*A Tour throughout the Whole Islands of Great Britain*':

> "... I know nothing else this town is remarkable for, except the most notorious smuggling trade, carried on partly by the assistance of the Dutch, in their oyster boats....the people hereabouts are arrived to such proficiency, that they are grown monstrous rich by that wicked trade".

For many though, there was a romanticism associated with smuggling, and this soon became a theme for many works of fiction. In 1845, George Payne Rainsford James wrote the hernia inducing three volume novel '*The Smuggler*', whilst in the early nineteen hundreds, Russell Thorndike created a series of novels around the aptly named character of Reverend Doctor Christopher Syn. His first, '*Dr Syn: A Tale of the Romney Marsh*' was set in the eighteenth century and, like Rudyard Kipling's poem, '*A Smuggler's Song*', captures something of the flavour of this clandestine operation. '*Moonfleet*', by John Meade Falkner went on to become a Fritz Lang film of the same name, whilst Ian Fleming brought such nefarious activities into modern times in '*Diamonds are Forever*'.

24

Wherever the setting, or whatever the period, would smuggling have even begun without those oystermen and their cargo of *Ostrea*?

In the mid nineteenth century, London was the largest city in the world as well as one of immense contrasts. The poor and destitute lived in close proximity to some of the wealthiest people in the country, and rag-clad urchins shared the streets with the well-heeled. With a thriving shop trade as well as multitudes of street sellers, streets were places to go to rather than go through. Street vendors were everywhere; hardly surprising when an estimated thirty thousand adults and innumerable children made their living in this way. They sold everything from ballads and broadsheets to violets and watercress, as well as services such as knife-grinding and repairing pots and pans. Of all the vendors though, it was probably those who sold food which were most important to the populace. For some Londoners buying a meal, however meagre, in the street was a matter of necessity as their overcrowded dwellings often lacked even the most basic cooking facilities. The better off though also regarded eating ready-prepared food as a normal adjunct to everyday life.

Hot potatoes, cooked eels, bread and pastries were all popular and filling, whilst oysters, whelks and winkles were seasonal treats cheap enough to be enjoyed by the poor. As Sam Weller noted in a conversation with Mr Pickwick in Dickens' '*Pickwick Papers*':

"Not a very nice neighbourhood this, sir" said Sam, with a touch of the hat, which always preceded his entering into conversation with his master.

"It is not indeed, Sam," replied Mr Pickwick, surveying the crowded and filthy street through which they were passing.

25

"It's a very remarkable circumstance, sir," said Sam, "that poverty and oysters always seems to go together."
"I don't understand, Sam," said Mr. Pickwick.

"What I mean, sir," said Sam, "is, that the poorer a place is, the greater call there seems to be for oysters. Look here, sir; here's a oyster stall to every half dozen houses. The streets lined vith 'em. Blessed if I don't think that ven a man's wery poor, he rushes out of his lodgings and eats oysters in reg'lar desperation."

'Reg'lar desperation' indeed must have been the lot of many of the men, women and children who sold shellfish. Whelk sellers began their day early so the snails could be boiled and cleaned of mud and dirt before they were drained and set out on saucers for sale. At the cost of one penny for a half dozen, the vendor would need a brisk trade to make a living wage. Periwinkles were more profitable and 'wink men' as they were called could make up to twelve shillings a week in the summer, though times were harder for them later in the year.

Eating oysters transcended class, for even though they were consumed in large quantities by the poor, they were also a favourite of men at the end of a visit to the theatre or a night's drinking. In the season 1848-1849, one hundred and eighty thousand bushels of oysters were sold in London. A bushel was the dry measure equivalent of eight gallons, so that means somewhere in the order of sufficient oysters to fill two and a half Olympic sized swimming pools. In terms of number, that equates to approximately fifty four million oysters. The entrepreneurial spirit of the Victorians is often cited as the reason behind London's pre-eminence in those times, but how much of it was also founded on the self-sacrifice of those oysters and the other molluscs in sustaining the workforce?

The nocturnal snacks of oysters consumed by the late night revellers might have been bought from a street vendor, but more usually they were sold in oyster houses which did their best business well into the early hours. Some customers chose to take their purchases away and eat them elsewhere, whilst others stood at the counter or went into a back room or one above the shop. If this sounds a little like what happens in towns and cities today, with kebab shops, fried chicken take-aways and Indian and Chinese restaurants satisfying the demands of late-night revellers, perhaps the custom can be traced back to those Victorian oyster houses.

It was far from 'reg'lar desperation' which caused Dr William Stephens, the Dean of Winchester to eat oysters in 1902. Instead they formed part of a banquet in honour of the mayor of that city where he had been Dean for the past seven years. The oysters he consumed had come from Emsworth, a village on the Hampshire coast for which it was famous.

Oysters, like other bivalve molluscs, feed on microscopic planktonic organisms by passing the water in which they live through their gills. Their gills act as a sort of sieve and trap their food, so it is a neat way of respiring and feeding at the same time. The animals do not select which organisms they will filter out, so if ones harmful to human health are present in the water, they will also be taken up. In nature there are a number of species of harmful phytoplankton, but human activity can make the problem much worse. Eating the infected shellfish could then lead to various forms of food poisoning, although in most cases these will not be fatal.

Until the Victorian times, most human waste went into earth closets or privies which were then emptied and the contents spread on the land as fertiliser. With the rise of cities though, these were gradually replaced with water closets which emptied into sewers. These sewers, in turn, ran into rivers, or in the case of seaside towns, directly into the sea. In the early 1900s, new sewers were installed in Emsworth, and these discharged onto the foreshore in the vicinity of the village's oyster farm. With no visible effects on the oysters, they continued to be harvested and some ended up at the mayoral banquet in Winchester. Unfortunately for Dr Stephens, at least one of them which he ate had filtered out typhoid bacteria, *Salmonella typhi*, the disease to which he succumbed a few days later.

Prior to the demise of Dr Stephens, many other people died of typhoid, with epidemics throughout the nineteenth century. Prince Albert may well have been a victim, but in those times diagnosis was uncertain and it was classed along with typhus and other diseases as 'continued fevers' as a cause of death. Not all who contracted the disease would have done so through eating contaminated shellfish, but eventually the danger to health through putting raw sewage into the sea was realised. Most sewage is now treated before it is discharged, but it took more outbreaks of shellfish poisoning, as well as a few of common sense by humans, to end the practice.

The fact that Giacomo Casanova lived to the age of seventy three suggests that the oysters he ate regularly were not contaminated with typhoid or any other form of poisoning. In his memoirs, he recorded that he ate fifty at breakfast. Born in Venice in 1725, he travelled widely in Europe and in 1774 was a spy in the Venetian service. His adventures alone might have made intriguing reading, but posterity remembers him as possibly the world's greatest lover, and Casanova admitted to having had one hundred and twenty two affairs. It is not for us molluscs to judge the morality of such behaviour, but human history is human history and Casanova ascribed his virility to oysters. Not surprisingly perhaps for as an aphrodisiac, their libido boosting powers were recognised at least as far back as the Romans.

Now before you dismiss their properties as fanciful, consider findings reported by Dr Antimo D'Aniello. When at the Laboratory of Neurobiology in Naples he analysed samples of bivalve molluscs for their amino acid content. Amino acids are the building blocks of proteins including hormones. Using liquid chromatography, he found two unusual ones, D-aspartic acid and N-methyl-D-aspartate. In earlier experiments, Dr D'Aniello found that injecting rats with these amino acids set off a chain of hormone production, culminating in increased levels of testosterone production in males and progesterone in the females. Increased levels of these hormones in the blood lead to an increase in sexual activity. So, according to Dr D'Aniello, oysters really are aphrodisiacs and it is thanks to the oysters that the phrase 'to be a Casanova' entered the English language.

4

'...and wrapped him in fine linen.'

In September 2006, Pope Benedict XVI stood in contemplation before a solid silver reliquary decorated with gold and precious stones. His attention was being given to an almost transparent piece of pale brown cloth measuring some twenty four centimetres high by eighteen centimetres wide, held behind two sheets of protective glass. As he reflected on it, he may well have been recalling a visit he made to see a much venerated and larger linen cloth a few years earlier. That the cloth before him was very old was beyond doubt, for it had been in the town since the start of the sixteenth century, but the material from which it had been made was, and remains, uncertain. To avoid damage, it has not been removed from the reliquary for scientific investigation, so all examinations have been only visual. On the basis of these, some authorities state that it is of linen whilst others support what we molluscs have long believed, that it is made of 'sea silk'.

Once more widely made, 'sea silk' was a fabric known for thousands of years, especially in the countries bordering the Mediterranean Sea. It is produced by the cleaning and combing of fine yet strong protein threads called byssus which the bivalve mollusc *Pinna nobilis* uses to anchor itself to the seabed. Unlike most bivalves, which lie buried in sand or mud, *Pinna* lives above the surface. It is commonly called the noble pen shell, but its scientific name provides a more accurate description. The generic name, *Pinna*, implies that its shells are shaped like a human ear, and at up to 120 centimetres in size, its specific name, *nobilis,* could not be more appropriate. It is the largest shellfish found only in the Mediterranean.

Life begins for it as a free-swimming larva, but after a few days of this planktonic existence, it grows a pair of calcareous shells and sinks to the seabed. Right away the animal produces its first byssal thread from a gland in its flexible, muscular foot. Using the tip of its foot, *Pinna* attaches the thread to a solid surface, often the roots of a seagrass plant, and once in contact with the seawater, the thread hardens. As the *Pinna* grows, so it produces more and more byssus, until its shells appear to be covered in a beard of golden thread. When taken from the sea and dried, these threads become a light brown colour and almost transparent. Today, as a result of overfishing, pollution and habitat change, *Pinna nobilis* is facing extinction, so whilst it is still possible to see this magnificent mollusc, let me explain why it has helped shape human history.

I cannot tell when humans first thought of using the byssus for producing cloth. *Pinna* shells have been found on sites from the Greek Bronze Age, but they might have been simply the remains of a meal. Certainly though it was being used for weaving by AD 200, when the Roman historian Tertullian wrote that:
> "... fleeces are obtained from the sea, where shells
> of extraordinary size are furnished with tufts of
> mossy hair."

Large numbers of *Pinna* need to be harvested to yield sufficient byssus to make a garment, so sea silk was a fabric only affordable by the wealthy. In about AD 500, the historian Procopius recorded that the emperor Justinian presented five satraps, or governors, of Armenia with cloaks made from it as a sign of power. Their cloaks were:

> *"...made of wool, not such as is produced by sheep, but gathered from the sea. Pinnoi the creature is called on which the wool grows."*

If cloth made from sea silk was used as a symbol of a person's wealth and influence during their lifetime, so too it could follow them into the grave. In ancient Jewish burials a small square of cloth known as a sudarium, and sometimes made of this material, was frequently placed over the face of the dead person and then their body was wrapped in many layers of linen. The higher the person's station in life, the finer the quality of the cloth used. Many scholars believe that after his crucifixion, Jesus was treated in this way:

> *"Joseph took Him down and wrapped Him in fine linen."* (Mark 15:46)

It has further been suggested that a sudarium was placed immediately onto his face, that a shroud was then used to cover his body, and a cloak was then wrapped around it. Finally another sudarium was fixed to the cloak above his face. According to John, after Jesus' resurrection, Simon Peter entered the tomb where:

> *"He saw the strips of linen lying there, as well as the burial cloth that had been around Jesus' head. The cloth was folded up by itself, separate from the linen."* (John 20: 5-7).

It is significant, I believe, that the strips of cloth are reported to have been made of linen, but no mention is made of the type of the material that was used to cover Jesus' head.

What subsequently happened to these various pieces of cloth has also exercised historians over the centuries. There are no early reliable records, but from the beginning of the fifteenth century, one large rectangular piece began to attract the attention of the church. It bore the image of a man wearing a crown of thorns and showing wounds consistent with having been scourged and crucified. Rather like an old and badly faded photographic negative, the overall form of the body was clear, but tantalisingly indistinct when it came to the fine details of his face. For many years it found resting places in churches and monasteries around Europe, drawing many pilgrims to see it and being the centre of controversy as to whether the face really was that of Jesus. Now known as the Shroud of Turin, after the city in which it is now kept within the Cathedral of St John, the Catholic Church has still not given its verdict on its authenticity. However, in the year 2000, after having made his own visit to see the Shroud, Cardinal Ratzinger wrote that it was:

"a truly mysterious image, which no human artistry was capable of producing."

Another, smaller piece of pale brown cloth arrived in the small Italian town of Manoppello in 1506, and in 1638 it was donated to the convent of the Capuchin Friars. It carried the image of a long haired man with a broken nose, a bloodstained forehead and a swollen cheek. In the latter part of twentieth century, a Trappist Nun, Sister Blandina Paschalis Schlöemer, obtained a photograph of the image of the face on the Turin Shroud and one of the Manoppello face. By superimposing transparencies of them, she claimed to find several points which aligned together perfectly. In her opinion, and that of many others, both pieces of cloth had been used to wrap the body of Jesus.

In contrast to the image on the Turin Shroud, the face on the veil of Manoppello is so clear that many have suspected that it is a painting, although recent research has not detected pigments on the cloth. Beneath well-defined brows, the eyes are open and alert, with dark brown irises. The man's mouth is open, revealing teeth in the upper jaw. His features are so clear that he would be recognisable if you passed him in the street. Little wonder that in September 2006 Pope Benedict XVI, or Cardinal Ratzinger as he had been until the previous year, stood before it in wonderment. Was he really beholding the image of Jesus, preserved over the centuries by a cloth made from the byssus of *Pinna nobilis*?

5

Born in the purple

When, on 12th April 1204, Andrew of Durebois stormed across a siege tower and onto the fortifications of Constantinople, he was probably more concerned with staying alive than considering the long term consequences of his action. Within a short time, many of the twenty thousand men who had been with him on the Venetian ships that made up the invasion fleet had joined him inside the city. They were Christian soldiers of the Fourth Crusade, a force assembled under the authority of Pope Innocent III, and whose purpose had been to recapture Jerusalem from the Moslems. For reasons that many humans cannot understand, and we molluscs certainly do not, they had chosen to attack Constantinople, the capital of the Christian Byzantine Empire, on the way. Whatever the motivation, on the following day Constantinople was sacked, vast quantities of gold, silver and jewels looted, and its population massacred. It was an event which solidified the schism between the Christian church in the East and the West, effectively ended the eight hundred year old Byzantine Empire, and saved millions of the mollusc *Murex* from a horrible death.

Murex is a genus of marine gastropods that resemble large, spiny whelks and which live on rocky shores around the Mediterranean Sea. Many gastropods are herbivorous, but *Murex* are carnivores and prey mainly on bivalve molluscs, and it was the understanding of their feeding habit and, more importantly the discovery of their valuable secretions, which led to their exploitation by humans. The secretion was processed into a purple pigment which was so expensive that an ancient civilisation became wealthy through it, and only the most wealthy could wear clothes which had been dyed with it.

According to the Roman mythographer, Julius Pollux, it was Heracles' dog that discovered the source of the dye. On the seashore of the Levant, that area which stretches from present day Turkey to Israel, it began playing with a living *Murex* which responded in the way they do when provoked – by producing a mucus secretion from beneath its shell. This, it was reputed, stained the dog's mouth purple. If this really was the case, then Heracles missed out on a superb business opportunity, leaving it to the Phoenicians to re-discover it and establish a dye trade which proved to be incredibly lucrative.

From at least 1600BC, the Phoenicians closely guarded the process by which they made their dye, and in doing so established the world's first large scale chemical industry. Other dyes were made at that time from both plant and animal sources but Tyrian Purple, as it became known, was far superior to them in that it was colour fast and did not fade in sunlight. Like many other industrial secrets over the centuries, it was the detail of manufacture which was crucial in maintaining their monopoly on production for so long.

It was not until the first century AD, by which time Phoenicia was under the auspices of the Roman Empire, that some idea of how it was made was written down. Pliny the Elder recorded that the dye's synthesis was based on *Murex*, and he explained how they were caught and processed. According to him, wicker baskets in the sea were baited with live bivalve molluscs which are the favourite food of *Murex.*

> *"The best time to catch them is after the rising of the dog-star or before spring arrives, for, when they have produced the honeycomb-like exudation, the juice is too thin."*

The snails crawled into the baskets to feed and these were then hauled up by the fishermen to meet their fate. When the Phoenicians first began to make the dye this was likely to have consisted of little more than throwing the unfortunate animals into large vats and leaving them to decompose. The resultant stench was so powerful that it was mentioned by ancient writers, so perhaps this explains Heracles' lack of interest in producing the dye. With one thousand cattle living in them, and not having been done for thirty years until he came along, cleaning the Augean stables had probably been more than sufficient for him. Humans with strong stomachs or no sense of smell would have removed the rotting mollusc broth from the vats and processing was ready to begin.

As production techniques became more refined, the Phoenicians discovered that it was the hypobranchial gland, a structure situated beneath the animal's mantle cavity, which secretes the mucus which is itself the precursor of the dye. Rather than using entire animals, the gland was extracted and put with a quantity of salt into large vessels. Sadly, this improved method was of no benefit to the *Murex.* After having been left to steep for three days the mixture underwent boiling and any fleshy remnants were skimmed off. Boiling continued for about ten days, the quantity of liquid gradually decreasing, until it was ready for quality testing. For this, a well washed fleece was then plunged in and the amount of dye taken up examined. By re-boiling and re-dipping, the end of the process could then be determined.

And what a costly process it was. In the fourth century BC, the Greek historian Theopompus wrote of its sale in a Roman city in present day Turkey:

"Purple for dyes fetched its weight in silver at Colophon".

The price paid by the *Murex* was worse. It has been estimated that twelve thousand animals gave less than one and a half grams of pure dye.

Two species of *Murex, Murex brandaris* and *Murex trunculus*, were used to produce the deep purple dye which was the most prized. By varying the relative amounts extracted from the two species, the degree of exposure to sunlight of the dye, and by mixing it with pigments taken from other molluscs, other shades from blue to pink could be created.

There is, in fact, dispute about the exact colour that 'Tyrian Purple' really was. Unlike the buildings which the ancient humans constructed or the weapons that they forged, and which gave historians tangible information about their early civilisations, clothing, and most certainly its colour, is ephemeral. Scholars are reliant on written descriptions of something which cannot be measured or quantified, so just what was the colour of Tyrian Purple?

To modern humans it suggests a colour not dissimilar to violet, but this may not always have been the case. The word itself is derived from the Latin '*purpura*', which in turn comes from the Greek 'πορφύρεος' or '*porphura*', and this is where it becomes complicated. Some of the earliest references to the colour are made by the Greek poet Homer, and he uses the word 'πορφύρεος' somewhat loosely to say the least. It describes both death and water and, I believe very significantly, blood and various forms of dyed cloth. Later writers seem to have attempted to clarify his meanings by looking at the context in which Homer used 'πορφύρεος', but in so doing just increased the misunderstandings. So, clothes dyed with Tyrian Purple may not really have been the shade that humans now understand by that name, but more the colour of dried blood. If this appears to be mere conjecture, then examine the sixth century mosaic of the Emperor Justinian in the Basilica of San Vitale in Ravenna. Unless the artist responsible for creating it was colour blind, or unable to obtain the correct colour of stones, then Justinian wore a toga which was blood coloured and not purple at all.

Putting the exact colour to one side, the Phoenicians and their Tyrian purple, or perhaps more accurately, their *Murex*, shaped the Classical Mediterranean world. Phoenicia was not really a country but a region made up of a number of city states, including Sidon, Byblos and Tyre, and galleys from Tyre crossed the Mediterranean Sea to ancient Greece.

In Homer's *Iliad*, when after a day's combat between Ajax and Hector a draw was declared, Hector gave Ajax a sharp sword as a gift, whilst Ajax returned the compliment with a purple sash. For such items to have been considered as of equal value illustrates the esteem in which the purple dye was held.

The blankets on Odysseus' wedding bed were of a similar hue, and when King Agamemnon returned from Troy he discovered his wife, Clytemnestra, had carried out a make-over of his palace in his absence and the carpets were now purple. A short time later, Agamemnon was murdered, some say by Clytemnestra and allegedly as revenge for him having sacrificed their daughter, Iphigenia, but I believe it could have equally well have been the result of a domestic dispute over the colour scheme. 'How much did you pay?' I can hear him demanding when he saw the bill.

At about the same time when Phoenicia was at the height of its influence, Moses was leading his people out of slavery in Egypt. On their way to the Promised Land they stopped off at the foot of Mt Sinai in the waterless wastes of the desert and Moses answered God's call to climb to the top of the mountain. Whilst on the summit he received the Ten Commandments which set out the principles by which the Israelites should live. He was also commanded to build a special tent, known as the tabernacle in which the Ark of the Covenant was to be housed. Instructions for its construction were very detailed, with the dimensions and the particular type of wood for the frame being specified. Even the fittings were not overlooked. Fabrics coloured with the blue and purple dyes from Tyre's *Murex* were integral to this:

> *"Make the tabernacle with ten curtains of finely twisted lined and blue, purple and scarlet yarn,..."* (Exodus 26:1)

Exact specifications were also laid down for priestly garments:

> *"Make them use gold, and blue, purple and scarlet yarn, and fine linen. "* (Exodus 28:5).

For the next three hundred years the tabernacle remained the centre of the nation's worship until it was replaced by the temple built by Solomon in Jerusalem. In an early example of an international trade deal, King Hiram of Tyre provided Solomon with cedar and pine for its construction, as well as a craftsman by the name of Huram-Abi.

"He is trained to work in gold and silver...and with purple and blue and crimson yarn and fine linen." (2 Chronicles 2:14).

In return King Hiram was sent large quantities of wheat, barley, wine and olive oil.

Huram-Abi was to work with Solomon's craftsmen and presumably was successful for inside the temple:
"He made the curtain of blue, purple and crimson yarn..." (2 Chronicles 3:14).

The tradition established by Moses and the multitude of unfortunate *Murex* continues to this day with blue tassels in the four corners of the Jewish prayer shawl and in the tapestries of the tabernacle.

By 15BC, Phoenicia had become a colony of Rome and any citizen wealthy enough to afford to do so could wear a toga to show their status, with the amount of purple on it being approximately equivalent to their social standing. A plain white toga signified someone who was freeborn, whilst a broad stripe on the border of the *'toga praetexta'* was the mark of a senator. Only those of even higher rank were permitted the solid purple *'toga picta'*. Embroidered with gold, this was worn by generals during their triumph in the days of the Roman republic, and later, during the Empire, it became the apparel of magistrates, consuls and emperors. Caligula, that emperor renowned for his mental stability and kindness, had the King of Mauritania assassinated for having a better purple cloak than his own. Through its association with the ruling classes, Tyrian Purple also became known as Royal purple and Imperial purple, and hence sons of reigning emperors were *"born in the purple"*.

As somewhere in the region of twelve thousand *Murex* were needed to produce less than one and a half grams of dye, and this was sufficient only for colouring the edging of one garment, how many must it have taken for a *toga picta*? How many millions must have been used to satisfy the demand of the Roman Empire? As far as all *Murex* were concerned, the fall of Constantinople could not have come quickly enough. With its vast wealth needed to afford them gone, the demand for their bodies also disappeared. Their numbers, decimated by centuries of overfishing, then began to crawl back from the edge of extinction, and Tyrian Purple would become a phrase consigned to the books of human history, but what a history it created!

Unsurprisingly stories of the Roman Empire have gripped human imagination right up to the present day. Hollywood Roman epic films such as *'Gladiator', 'Quo Vadis'* and *'The Fall of the Roman Empire'* cost millions of dollars to produce and attempted to recreate the appearance of the time. Expensive sets were constructed and costumes designed to look authentic. The senators, generals and emperors all wore their togas showing the appropriate amount of purple, and this is where the Homeric confusion reappears. In *'Quo Vadis'*, Nero wore a distinctly un-Tyrian purple toga, as did Antony in *'Cleopatra'*. The costume department of the BBC seem to have done better though and on a smaller budget. In their comedy series *'Up Pompeii'*, Nero's toga was much nearer in colour to the maroonish purple that he probably wore in real life. For any of these films, however, the costumes would have been created using modern, synthetic dyes, the result of painstaking work by chemists. No *Murex* were harmed in these productions!

Although the Phoenicians were the undoubted experts in manufacturing their dye from *Murex*, they had no idea of the complex chemistry involved. This had to wait until the beginning of the twentieth century, when the chemist Paul Friedländer discovered the main constituent of Tyrian Purple was a molecule called 6,6'-dibromoindigo. It took even longer for scientists to work out how it ended up being produced from the starting point of the *Murex*. The Phoenicians were correct in using the hypobranchial gland, for this makes a colourless secretion containing indoxyl sulphate. A series of chemical changes then take place, producing compounds of various colours, but ending up with a green one called tyriverdin. In the presence of light, this then forms the 6,6'-dibromoindigo, along with the highly odorous by-product dimethyl disulfide. Just as we will never know for certain the shade that was Tyrian Purple, neither will we know exactly what was the stench given off in its production. Perhaps the smell noted by the ancient writers was more than just rotting *Murex* flesh after all, and was actually the rotting cabbage smell of dimethyl disulphide. Whatever it was, it was enough to put off Heracles from cashing in on his dog's understanding of advanced organic chemistry.

6

"We weren't going to attack it with our penknives."

Olivier de Kersauson de Pennendreff is a man whose length of name was exceeded only by his desire to set a world record for circumnavigating the globe in a sailing ship in the shortest time. In January 2003, in his enormous ocean-going trimaran named *Geronimo*, the French sailor left the starting point, an imaginary line between the Lizard lighthouse in England and Ouessant Island, France, and headed into the Atlantic. All went without incident until in the middle of the night and the vessel was off Madeira, when it began to shudder as if it had run aground. Using torches to allow them to see what had happened, the crew were astonished to find the hulls were in the embrace of thick tentacles, and two were wrapped around the rudder, causing it to bend. As reported on the BBC News website: *"We didn't have anything to scare off the beast [...] We weren't going to attack it with our penknives."*

Olivier de Kersauson had spent the best part of his life crossing the world's oceans, so was no stranger to the natural phenomena that could be encountered, but this was something beyond his experience. From the thickness of the glistening tentacles, he and his crew could only conclude that what was holding them back was a giant squid, estimated to be thirty feet (ten metres) in length. Few people have seen a living Giant squid, *Architeuthis,* but they were convinced that is what it was. After a few minutes the animal – the second largest living invertebrate after the Colossal squid – released its grip, and the vessel was able to continue on its voyage. de Kersauson did not use this encounter as a reason for his failing to establish a new sailing record, but in the following year, without molluscan interference, he accomplished the feat. It seemed both fitting and ironic that de Kersauson should have been competing for the Jules Verne trophy, named in honour of the author.

That de Kersauson came across a Giant squid off Madeira is not particularly surprising as the animals seem to prefer the waters of continental and island slopes. What is more unusual though is that it was on the surface, for under normal circumstances they inhabit the ocean depths, down as far as one thousand metres. Dwelling so deep in the sea has meant that scientists know relatively little about their biology, and until fairly recent times even their very existence was a question for debate.

That debate was very much to the fore when in November 1861, the French corvette *Alecton* was cruising between Madeira and Tenerife when a lookout spotted one swimming on the surface. Brick red in colour, its length was estimated at sixteen to eighteen feet (five to six metres), excluding its tentacles. The *Alecton*'s commander gave orders to try to capture it, and the ship's cannon and harpoons were made ready. During the course of the following three hours, the animal was struck by several cannon balls, but without any obvious effect, whilst the harpoons that penetrated it came out of its rubbery body without fixing. Eventually a lasso was thrown around its body and made fast in front of its fins. The crew then began to haul the squid out of the water, but as its buoyancy became lost, so the rope penetrated into the animal's flesh, eventually cutting it in two. The bulk of the body slipped back into the sea and was lost, and the remaining hind portion, though brought on board, was not preserved. Scientists were therefore unable to study the animal, but the officers' words were accepted and became one of the first credible accounts of the existence of the Giant squid.

This incident was definitely known to the French author Jules Verne. In 1870 he published his novel *Twenty Thousand Leagues Under The Sea*, which followed the journey of the submarine *Nautilus* under the command of Captain Nemo. Also aboard were Professor Aronnax, his servant Conseil, and the harpoonist Ned Land. At one point in the narrative, Verne had Conseil and Ned Land discussing the *Alecton*'s capture of the Giant squid, followed soon after by coming face to face with one themselves. Verne provided a graphic description of the animal although, possibly reflecting the lack of knowledge about them at that time, gave it two hundred and fifty air holes on the inner side of its tentacles. When a total of seven Giant squid began to attack the *Nautilus*, Captain Nemo made the decision to bring his submarine to the surface and kill them. In so doing, one of his crew was carried off by the squid, but eventually the boat was freed and they continued on their voyage,

Squid are certainly carnivorous, but their normal prey are other species of squid and deep sea fish, rather than humans, and the likelihood of them attacking a submarine in such an organised manner is highly implausible. Nevertheless, Jules Verne told a gripping story, even though he portrayed the squid as villains, and it subsequently spawned numerous adaptations in a range of genre.

The most memorable interpretation is probably the 1954 Walt Disney film of the same name. The first science fiction film to be shot in CinemaScope, it had audiences transfixed by the many dramatic scenes, and of all of these, that featuring the fight with the Giant squid is the most spectacular. To create this, a mechanical squid was constructed, but so clumsy was its movements that the first attempt at filming had to be scrapped. The sequence was then re-shot, but this time at night and during a violent storm, in order to hide the system of levers, cables and hydraulics that operated it. One thing that the production team did not hide though was the mechanical squid's beak. Superficially resembling that of a parrot, the upper part of squid's beak fits into the lower half, whilst with a parrot, the lower part fits into the upper. Presumably no-one mentioned they had it the wrong way round! It may be just a small matter to humans, but we molluscs do not want to be misrepresented. I have been told that there had been several Giant squid willing to take on the role, but Kirk Douglas, as Ned Land, was unwilling to play opposite any of them. Perhaps he was following the old acting dictum of never to perform alongside children or animals for fear of being upstaged.

Sea monsters to be feared date back well before the advent of cinema or even of Jules Verne, and in 1752, Bishop Pontoppidan of Bergan published an account of the legendary kraken, based on the testimony of Norwegian fishermen who claimed they were well acquainted with it. Pontoppidan wrote that its body was about one and a half miles in circumference, and with arms of such strength that they could drag the largest man-of-war beneath the waves. On submerging, the water that its vast body had displaced then rushed in like a whirlpool so powerful that it could drag any vessel down with it. I sense some degree of exaggeration in all of this, but then I believe fishermen are prone to embellishing sizes when it comes to aquatic life. Most probably what they had seen were Giant squids which can reach a length of fourteen metres and weigh up to seven hundred and fifty kilograms; far less than Bishop Pontoppidan's claim, but sufficient to fuel the imagination of frightened fishermen in small boats far from the safety of land.

As the chilly waters of the Norwegian coast were the home of the kraken, so the warmer climes of Greece was where the equally mythical Hydra was said to have been found, and just as the fertile human imagination created a monster out of the Giant squid, so I believe it conceived the Hydra from another mollusc.

Being mythical, it is of no surprise that there is no definitive description of the animal, and over the centuries, since it first emerged in ancient times, writers have given it different attributes. All agree it had a large body and is most usually considered to have had eight mortal heads, and a ninth immortal one. It lived in the marshes of Lerna in the present day Greek administrative area of Argolis, and sometimes searched out and ate cattle living in the surrounding land. For his second labour, Heracles was required to kill the beast, which he attacked with a sickle, sword or club depending on whose version of the story you choose. Unfortunately whatever the weapon, whenever one head was cut off, at least two more grew in its place, and Hydra would only die when it lost its last head. Faced with an apparently impossible task, help came in the form of Heracles' nephew Iolaus who used a flaming torch to burn the stumps and prevent the new heads from growing. Eventually he severed the final head with a blow from the golden sword given to him by Athena and the Hydra was no more.

I came across this story when I found a book about Heracles' twelve labours in the library belonging to the aquarium in which I was living at the time. Now that fact alone is significant in my postulation that Hydra was based on a mollusc, or more specifically an octopus, for I had to escape from my tank, cross the floor of the aquarium, and then pass through the open door into the adjacent library. You may find that hard to believe, but there are many video clips available which show other octopuses "walking" by using their tentacles as legs, though it was an ability also known to the Greeks. Back in 350BCE, Aristotle wrote in Book IX of *The History of Animals* that: *"The octopus is the only mollusc that ventures on to dry land; it walks by preference on rough ground;"*. The cattle which the Hydra was reputed to eat would be too big to be preyed on by an octopus, but the principle is clear enough.

The seas around the Greek coast abound with octopus, so the ancient Greeks would have been totally familiar with them. They were portrayed on vases, coins and broaches, and some ornaments were even in the shape of the animal itself. That an octopus has eight arms and Hydra had eight mortal ones is just too much of a similarity to be dismissed as coincidence, whilst how they employ them is also the same. According to Appolodorus writing in the first century BCE in his *Library book two*, after Heracles had forced the Hydra to leave its den it then: *"wound itself about one of his feet and clung to him."* This is exactly the way in which an octopus uses its arms to grip its prey, and with immense power too. Ancient Greeks reported cases where octopuses came out of the water onto jetties and crushed wooden barrels with their arms to get at the fish contained inside. Such a prodigious feat would make them a worthy adversary for Heracles.

One final, and I think decisive similarity between the mythical Hydra, and the very real octopus is their power of regeneration. That of Hydra would have been spectacular had it been true, yet that of the octopus is almost as amazing, and the Greeks had observed it for themselves. Few octopuses living in the wild have all eight arms intact, having lost parts to various predators including toothed whales and conger eels, but within a few weeks, the injured arm is back to normal. What the Greeks would not have known is how it happened.

Recent research is moving towards an explanation. In part it is due to the lack of any internal skeleton which would require rebuilding, but also to the presence of high levels of a protein called acetylcholinesterase. Researchers found that three days after the tip of an arm had been cut off, groups of undifferentiated cells began to form in the area of the stump. By the second week, blood vessels were forming at the site, and over the next one hundred days the muscles, nerves and the rest of the arm re-formed, including its suckers. At the time when the nerves were re-growing, high levels of acetylcholinesterase were found in the surrounding tissues, leading the researchers to conclude that this enzyme could have an important influence on the arm's regeneration. Acetylcholinesterase is also found in the nervous system of humans, so this new knowledge gained from the octopus could have a clear application in the field of regenerative medicine for humans. If this proves to be the case the scientists who made this discovery will receive due credit, but I have the feeling that no mention will be made of the molluscs who played their part in the work.

7

"...And many a conche on his cloke..."

In AD 44, on the orders of Herod Agrippa, a man called James was beheaded in Jerusalem. For several years previously, he had been preaching about Jesus on the Iberian peninsula, another region at that time, as was Jerusalem, under the control of the Roman Empire. Returning to his homeland was a career move with mixed benefits. In the short term it resulted in his death, but some years later James was to become recognised as a martyr for his faith. To avoid confusion, and to distinguish him from the other Apostle with the same Christian name, Saint James the Less, the one now less his head, was called Saint James the Greater. I hope that is clear, but if not, ask a human.

James' execution took place far from the sea and an even greater distance from Europe, but by means human or mystical, his body eventually found its way to the North West coast of Spain and where molluscs were then able to play their part in the development of the Christian church.

The origin of their involvement is lost in the spindrift of time, but one account tells of James' body being washed ashore, miraculously undamaged, but covered with scallops. This sounds highly implausible to me, as scallops do not attach themselves to rocks, let alone to a dead body, clothed or naked, of a human. *Pecten*, as the genus of these

51

bivalve molluscs is known, normally live on a sandy or shingly sea bed and have the rare ability amongst bivalves of being able to swim. They do so by snapping their shells together, a bit like water-filled castanets, so that the water expelled shoots them along by a type of jet-propulsion. Behaviourally, mussels would have been a much more likely group of molluscs to have attached themselves to St James' corpse, as they fix their shells to anything solid using strong protein threads of byssus, rather like *Pinna*. Their shells, however, lacked the potential for the symbolism that humans have ascribed to those of *Pecten*, as I will explain shortly, so it was *Pecten* shells which became firmly associated with the martyr.

With or without shells attached, his followers then transported James' body a short way inland to the town of Compostela for burial, and where a shrine was subsequently constructed. From the eighth century onwards, people crossed from all parts of Europe to visit this now venerated site of Santiago de Compostela; a pilgrimage which in those times ranked alongside those made to Rome or Jerusalem itself.

The first French pilgrimage took place in AD951, with the bishop of Le Puy at its head. In the years which followed, millions of Jacquets, Jacquots or Jacobites, as they called themselves, followed in his footsteps. To help the travellers, the world's first tourist guide, '*The Pilgrim's Guide*', was written in about AD1135. Produced in Latin, it must have had a severely limited readership, but for those able to understand it, there was information about the weather they might encounter as well as places of interest to visit on the way.

As a journey, it was an arduous and dangerous undertaking, but with absolution of sins as a reward at the end it was clearly worthwhile for many living in those times. So popular did the pilgrimages become, that a cathedral on the site of St James' grave was started in AD 1078. Today it is a World Heritage Site and an archiepiscopal see, and Compostela itself is a city of 95,000 inhabitants, yet without the scallops, it might have remained a small, sleepy Spanish town, and *Rough Guides* might never have been thought of.

It was not long after the pilgrimages began that *Pecten* became inextricably linked with them. In part this was symbolic. *Pecten*'s shells are strongly ribbed, radiating out from a single point, and in the same way, the multitude of routes which crossed Europe all converged on the shrine of Santiago de Compostela. Pilgrims from England might have travelled overland across the length of France, or made a shorter journey and arrived at Soulac on the west coast by ship before continuing on foot. Others would have walked all the way from their homes as far away as Poland, Moravia and Hungary.

Sanctuaries for these travellers were established at many towns along the route, with those at Tours, Poitiers and Angoulême being particularly important. Many would have made their last halt at St Jean Pied du Port before embarking on the exhausting climb across the Pyrenees. Their association with Saint James, together with the fact that *Pecten* shells could be found easily on the adjacent Spanish coast, soon made them also tangible symbols of a completed pilgrimage on the Camino de Santiago or The Way of St James.

There was a practical element to the scallop shell too. Fixed to the pilgrims' clothing or carried in their baggage, the shells were more than mere souvenirs. They marked out the wearer as a godly person and someone who was simply passing through a town or village and meant no harm. Should they need lodgings for the night, their host knew they were trustworthy and would require only a modest meal. Perhaps that meal would have been eaten out of the shell serving as a makeshift bowl, or used as a scoop and cup for drinking water.

Whether symbolic or practical, the scallop shell became an indispensable part of the pilgrimage. As William Langland wrote in his fourteenth century poem '*Piers Plowman*':

"A bolle and a bagge
He bar by his syde
And hundred ampulles
On his hat seten
Signes of Synay,
And Shelles of Galice,
And many a conche
On his cloke..."

A conche was the Medieval name for a shellfish, derived from the Latin word 'concha', but the shell's pilgrimage legacy lives on into modern times. Along the same routes tramped by ancient feet can be seen churches and abbeys with scallops carved into the stonework, signifying places where the pilgrims would have rested. And for those who still wish to follow the paths, there are often modern ceramic or self-adhesive markers bearing the motif stuck on posts to show the way. Seventeen English peers and eight baronets incorporate *Pecten* shells into their coats of arms as a consequence of their ancestors having made that journey.

Pecten's legacy in Spain does not just lie in Compostela. In the year AD884, so the legend goes, the Christian king Ramiro I of Leon was doing battle against the Muslims led by the Emir of Cordoba at Clavijo near Logroño in north eastern Spain. Things were not going the Christians' way until the miraculous intervention of Saint James. Riding a white horse with trappings covered in scallop shells, he slew sixty thousand of the king's enemies with his sword and carried the day. Hardly the sort of action that I would have expected from a saint, but perhaps he was still feeling bitter about having his own head cut off. Be that as it may, St James became the patron saint of Galicia and eventually of Spain, and it was under his banner that from the ninth century the Christians began to expel the Muslims from Iberia. In Spain today July 25th is a public holiday to celebrate the Feast Day of St James the Great.

Taking its name from the battling saint, the Spanish order of knighthood, Santiago de Espada – St James of the Sword – was founded in the twelfth century. The men of this order continued with the fight against the Muslims until their eventual expulsion following the battle at Granada in AD1492, as well as offering protection and hospitality to pilgrims passing along The Way of St James. Fittingly their symbol is a red sword, representing St James' blood stained one, and a white scallop shell. How different Europe might have been today had it not been for St James and, of course, *Pecten*.

Since at least the days of John the Baptist, washing with water has been used as a means of cleansing a person of their sins and marking the beginning of a new life. In the early days of Christianity this was usually conducted through total immersion, and although this practice is still carried out by some churches, baptism gradually became more symbolic. Small amounts of water are poured over the head of the person being baptised from a suitable vessel, which in many cases is shaped like a scallop shell. Some say that the shell just happens to be a convenient shape for scooping water, much as the pilgrims to Compostela found it. Others attest that the ribs of the shell represent the rays of the rising sun and the beginning of a new dawn; the first day of a new life for the person being baptised.

I personally favour the latter explanation because the shell of *Pecten* features in so many works of art which depict the baptism of Jesus. In Piero della Francesca's work, the *'Baptism of Christ'*, John the Baptist is shown pouring water over the head of Jesus. The surrounding scenery resembles Italy much more than the parched lands around the river Jordan, but the *Pecten* shell he is using is wonderfully accurate. So also is it in Murillo's *'The Baptism of Christ'*, and in that of the same title by El Greco. Now I am no connoisseur of human art, but I would consider El Greco's use of *Pecten* in his painting to be masterful. Here the water arcs out from the gentle curve of the scallop shell in John's hand and down unto Jesus' hair. In reality, a jug might be a more practical means of holding and pouring the water, but the iconography of the seashell is far more satisfying than a piece of shaped and baked clay.

As baptism inside a church became increasingly the norm, so a font became necessary as a place at which the ceremony could take place. Some early ones were like small baths sunk into the floor, but others took the form of basins on pedestals or were fixed to a wall. Rarely were the fonts plain, so what did the craftsmen who made them choose for decoration? In many cases it was the shells of *Pecten*. Four large scallop shells, one on each face of a square bowl, adorn the font in St. Audoen's Church in Dublin, whilst a frieze of more stylised scallops intertwine with other devices around that in the Clemenskirche in Wissel, Germany. In St Peter's church in Prickwillow, Cambridgeshire stands yet another fine example dating from the seventeenth century. And when the font is positioned against a wall, the recess in which it is located is often ornamented into the form of a scallop shell, as in the church of San Antonio de Padua in Izamal, Mexico. Representation of no other animal would work half as well.

Before I leave the subject of *Pecten*'s influence in art, I should mention one final painting by Botticelli which is probably his most famous work, and is regarded by many as one of the finest of the Renaissance. On display in the Uffizi gallery in Florence, *'The Birth of Venus'* shows the goddess having arisen from the sea as a fully grown woman, arriving on a sea shore. She is depicted standing inside an enormous scallop shell and riding a gentle swell, a bit like a modern day surfboarder who had inadvertently forgotten to put on her swimsuit. When I first saw it, I was delighted that the artist had chosen to place Venus on a sea shell when there are so many other creatures which could have brought her ashore, and particularly pleased with his skilful rendition of *Pecten*. Somewhat naively I assumed his choice of a mollusc shell had been based on its physical qualities such as its size, shape and seaworthiness, but it seems that this was not the case. Since Classical times, a seashell has been used as a symbol for that part of the goddess' anatomy which, at the moment he painted her, had been covered by a windblown lock of long hair. How convenient was that?

Back in 1833, a London businessman by the name of Marcus Samuel felt the time was right to expand his interests. Until then he had been selling antiques, but with the rising fashion of using seashells in interior design – a style I strongly disapprove of – he saw an opportunity of importing more exotic forms from the Far East. So began Marcus Samuel's import and export business, which in due course passed to his two sons, Marcus Samuel junior and Sam. Marcus Samuel senior might have been a good businessman but he does seem to have been a bit short on originality when it came to naming his children. Their names, however, were no handicap and soon they were showing themselves to be astute entrepreneurs in their own right.

Towards the end of the nineteenth century, oil was used as a lubricant and for lighting, but the invention of the internal combustion engine triggered a rise in its demand as a fuel. As now, much of it came from the Middle East, and in 1892 the Samuel brothers revolutionised its transport through the introduction of the world's first purpose built oil tanker, the *Murex*. What an appropriate name they chose for their vessel since *Murex* is that genus of sea mollusc I wrote about in chapter five. Indeed, further tankers owned by the company, called The Tank Syndicate, were named after other sea dwelling molluscs.

By 1897 the company was thriving and changed its name to The Shell Transport and Trading Company. To reflect its new name, some four years later, the Samuels adopted a mussel shell as their new company's logo. Now there is nothing wrong with mussels as molluscs as I have mentioned earlier, but as a symbol of pilgrimage, and certainly as a corporate image, they are not particularly memorable. In fact at a quick glance they do not look much more than a small piece of blue stone. Perhaps the Samuels could have used the name to good effect in their advertising with something along the lines of '*With mussel in your tank you'll have muscle in your engine*', but as far as I know they did not. Advertising though became increasingly important as competition between fuel companies grew ever more intense, so in 1904 they decided a different brand image was necessary and they decided on using *Pecten*.

At first the new logo was quite naturalistic, but from the 1930s onwards it became increasingly stylised with changes in graphic design. Colour was introduced to make it more eye-catching, and the bright red and yellow on petrol station forecourts certainly did that. But the chosen colours probably had more significance than mere visual attraction. They were introduced in California, a state with strong Hispanic connections, and red and yellow just happen to be the colours of the Spanish flag.

The choice of any seashell as the company's logo was in itself logical enough and *Pecten* is an instantly recognisable one, but there was more to its choice than mere chance; a choice which takes us right back to Santiago de Compostela. One of the company's customers in India was a certain Mr Graham. He not only bought large quantities of their fuel, but also invested in the company, and Mr Graham had *Pecten* as part of his family's coat of arms. At some time in the past Mr Graham's ancestors, possibly carrying a scallop shell attached to their clothing as a symbol of their pilgrimage, had trudged the arduous Camino de Santiago.

8

"Precious the tear ...Which turns into pearls..."

Historians will probably never agree about the reason that in 55BC Julius Caesar and his Roman legions invaded Britain. Some will say it was for the natural resources such as timber and tin, which he knew could be found there. Others will argue it was simply to enlarge the boundaries of the empire and enhance his prestige. We molluscs, however, know that it was accounts of pearls produced by the oysters and mussels of the country's seas and rivers which induced him. Sadly for Julius Caesar the rumours were without substance, and those pearls which were found proved to be small and of little value as gems. Tacitus was of the opinion that British pearls had:

"A cloudy and livid hue"

The dice had been cast though, and once they arrived, it would be several hundred years before the Romans left Britain. During that time they totally transformed the way of life of the inhabitants, and gained some consolation for failing to find good pearls by discovering that the oysters actually made exceptional eating.

At the time of Julius Caesar, the Roman Empire was vast, stretching from Spain in the West to Syria in the East, and from the cold climes of Britain to the sun-baked lands of North Africa. Even the ancient and powerful kingdom of Egypt came under its sway, and in 48BC, Julius Caesar arrived in Alexandria, the power base of the Ptolemy's. It was in this city that he encountered, and was captivated by, Cleopatra. He was fifty two years old and she twenty years his junior. Had Julius Caesar not made the mistake of attending a meeting of the senate in Rome on the morning of 15th March 44BC, his relationship with her might well have continued. Instead he was assassinated and at his funeral, a fellow consul called Antony gave the oration. These two Roman generals were both fixated by the same woman, yet in most people's minds it is Antony who is usually the more associated with Cleopatra.

Following Julius Caesar's death, leadership of the Roman Empire was shared between Antony and the increasingly powerful consul, Octavian. Octavian controlled the western portion with Spain and Gaul, whilst Antony ruled the eastern part, including Cleopatra's Egypt. Three years later Cleopatra was summoned by Antony to meet him in Tarsus. She was determined to maintain her country's relative independence from Rome and to do so, she believed, would require her to have power over Antony. Immediately she set out to seduce him and she succeeded magnificently, or as the historian Appian wrote:

"As soon as he saw her, Antony lost his head to her, as if he was a young man, although he was forty years old."

Stories of their extraordinary lives over the next five years became legendary and have been passed down to the present day through Shakespeare's play and Hollywood films. In rooms hung with tapestries interwoven with gold threads and filled with costly perfumes, their extravagance seemed to know no bounds. Following days of lavish feasting, Cleopatra proposed a bet with her lover that she could consume ten million sesterces in a single supper. The claim seemed so outrageous that Antony accepted the bet, and the meal was arranged for the following day.

The supper was, as expected, sumptuous, but not anywhere near sufficiently so to have cost the wagered sum. Antony must have felt he had won the bet and was demanding to see the accounts for the meal, but it was at that stage when, according to Pliny the Elder in his *Natural History* that:

> "...the attendants placed before her only one vessel of vinegar..."

It so happened that Cleopatra was wearing in her ears:

> "...two pearls, the very largest that ever were known in any age..."

She removed one of them and dropped it into the vessel, allowed it to react with the vinegar until it had liquefied, and then drank the resulting mixture. Had the adjudicator not intervened and declared that Antony had already lost his bet, she was ready to dissolve the second one. Personally, I think there are aspects of this episode which are highly unlikely, but I will explain why later on.

As much as the lives of Antony and Cleopatra were entwined, so too were the power politics of Rome and Egypt. According to Plutarch, Antony was:

> "carried away by her to Alexandria, there to keep holiday, like a boy, in play and diversion, squandering and fooling away in enjoyment that most costly of all valuables, time".

Whilst Antony was enjoying his luxurious lifestyle and his military skills atrophied, so his enemies in Rome were strengthening their positions. Matters came to a head on 2nd September 31BC when the fleets of Antony and

Cleopatra clashed with that of Octavian in the battle of Actium. How different the outcomes for Rome and Egypt might have been had Antony not been seduced by Cleopatra, gold and, of course, her pearls. Octavian, the victor, is better remembered as Augustus, the first of the Roman emperors and only one year later, after the deaths of the two great lovers, Egypt itself was annexed by Rome.

Most of the pearls so valued by the Romans and Egyptians came from oysters in the Red Sea or the Indian Ocean, where the lives of the men who collected them were dangerous and short. As if the prospect of being attacked by a shark whilst in the water was not bad enough, the very act of diving could be fatal. To be able to stay beneath the sea for longer, they would firstly hyperventilate. By taking repeated rapid breaths this would top up the oxygen dissolved in their blood, but also flush out more carbon dioxide. When the body respires, so the carbon dioxide level rises and this is then detected by a part of the brain. When it reaches a certain level it triggers the feeling which all humans experience when they try to hold their breath, the need to breathe again. Having hyperventilated, the divers would not feel that sensation as quickly and by the time they did, their oxygen levels would have dropped to below the level needed to sustain consciousness. Consequently they would pass out whilst surfacing and might well drown.

The diver, naked except for a pair of gloves to protect his hands when collecting the oysters, stood in a loop of rope to which was attached a very heavy stone. The other end of the rope was tied to the boat, and when the diver was ready, the free end was then released, swiftly taking him down to the sea bed. For as long as his breath held out, he filled a bag with oysters until he tugged on the rope to which the bag was fixed. This was then hauled up, leaving the diver to ascend on his own. It was reported that the men worked in water as deep as ninety feet, so the effect of a pressure of almost four times that of atmospheric on their bodies can only be imagined. Trauma to their eyes and ears was the least of their troubles and most died from damage to their lungs. To survive such a way of life for more than six years would have been exceptional.

Neither the people who fished for the oysters, nor the Romans, knew how the precious pearls were formed. Pliny the Elder recorded the belief that they were made by drops of rain falling into oyster shells whilst they were open. The rain drops then became hardened into pearls by some secretions of the animal. The Persians thought similarly, although they considered it was spring rain which was responsible. Thomas Moore captured the ideas of both civilisations when he penned the lines:

"Precious the tear as that rain from the sky
Which turns into pearls as it falls on the sea."

In as much as the pearl is made by the oyster itself, the Romans and Persians were correct, although something more substantial than a raindrop is needed to begin its formation. Let me explain.

Almost any mollusc with a shell can create a pearl, but it is only those from bivalve molluscs that humans value. The animal's soft body lies within the pair of protective shells, and is separated from them by a layer of tissue called the mantle. Foreign particles are usually prevented from getting between the mantle and the shell by a muscle which holds the two together. Occasionally though, when the shells are open for feeding or respiration, a parasite, piece of organic material, or even a grain of sand does enter. This then acts as the stimulus for the mantle to form a pearl, which is a natural reaction to seal off the potentially harmful irritant.

The mantle is not just responsible for making a pearl. It also lays down the shell itself, and whilst the outer surface may often appear dull, the inner one usually has a colourful sheen, known as mother-of-pearl. Mother-of-pearl and pearls themselves are made of layers of a form of the mineral calcium carbonate called aragonite, along with an organic material known as conchiolin, which binds them together. Collectively the aragonite and conchiolin form nacre, and in pearls it is the manner in which the nacre affects light which gives them their distinctive appearance. Concentric layers are built up, and through light's reflection the pearl gains its lustre, whilst refraction, or bending of the light rays, produces its shining iridescence.

Because they are naturally occurring, pearls vary greatly in their perceived quality. They are rare finds in themselves, but most are not the highly prized perfectly spherical ones. Any movement of the pearl within the shell as it is being formed will result in its deformation, whilst changes in the deposition of the nacre will influence the sheen and size. Little wonder then that huge numbers of oysters have to be opened and killed, just to find even one pearl that could be used as a jewel. Generally at least a tonne of oysters is required to yield just three or four of quality.

When the first European explorers arrived on the shores of the Americas, they were surprised, and no doubt delighted, to see the native people wearing fine pearls. They had not only discovered their New World, but also a new source of riches. Within a short time they had found out the locations of the oyster beds and were sending the pearls back to Spain to add to its rapidly increasing wealth.

Cities like New Cadiz on the island of Cubagua, off the coast of Venezuela, sprang up near to the beds, but such was their over-exploitation that by the end of the sixteenth century, the trade had virtually ceased. Along with the neighbouring island of Margarita, Cubagua's fortunes waned to nothing. Scarcity, it seemed, would dictate price, and pearls would seemingly always remain the preserve of the rich.

That was until William Saville-Kent and three Japanese men came along and between them made quality pearls affordable to others. William Saville-Kent was an expatriate Englishman working as a marine biologist in Australia during the late nineteenth century. Whilst there he hit upon the method of creating spherical cultured pearls, something that was eluding Kokichi Mikimoto in Japan. Mikimoto was already running a pearl oyster farm, but his pearls were not spheres and his business was not prospering. Two other Japanese, Tatsuhei Mise and Tokichi Nishikawa, met Saville-Kent when they were in Australia and he passed on to them the secrets of his technique. Both men returned to Japan, eventually cooperating in making spherical pearls through the 'Mise-Nishikawa method'. Perhaps they were less business minded than Mikimoto, for he then adopted their method, and from the first quarter of the twentieth century, his enterprise expanded rapidly. Today the term 'Mikimoto pearls' is almost synonymous with high quality yet, arguably, affordable pearls.

I have already explained how a pearl is formed naturally, and culturing them involves putting a nucleus into the mantle of the oyster and then letting nature do its work. The nucleus is usually a small piece of shell from a freshwater mussel and, depending on the type of oyster used, the pearl is removed from one to four years later. *Pinctada martensii* was the first oyster to be used by the Japanese for culturing pearls and grows only to eight centimetres in size. Its pearls, known as akoya pearls, are therefore usually less than ten millimetres diameter. Larger pearls are grown inside the South Pacific oysters *Pinctada maxima* and *Pinctada margaritifera*.

Superficially, a cultured pearl looks the same as a natural one, but x-ray examination will quickly reveal the difference inside. In a natural one, the layers of nacre form concentric rings around a solid core, whilst those of a cultured pearl follow the shape of the nucleus in its centre. Another clue might be how they are displayed. As they are so rare, natural pearls are usually set as centrepieces in a piece of jewellery, whilst a string of pearls is almost certain to be of cultured ones. The possession of many pearls in man's modern world is no longer a sign of wealth – which brings me back to Cleopatra and her dissolving pearl earring.

As I explained earlier, pearls are made of over 85% calcium carbonate, a mineral which reacts with an acid to produce carbon dioxide gas and a soluble salt. Vinegar, into which she was alleged to have dropped her pearl, is a 5-7% solution of acetic acid, but this is nowhere near sufficiently strong to dissolve an enormous pearl during a banquet unless it lasted for many days. Even Pliny had his suspicions that all was not as it seemed:

> "Cleopatra must have employed a stronger vinegar than that which we now use for our tables, as the pearls, on account of their hardness and natural enamel, cannot easily be dissolved by a weak acid."

If he was correct, the results would have been speedier and quite dramatic, and not only on the pearl. Unless she had been able to judge the correct volume of acid in which to dissolve her pearl to create a neutral solution, as she swallowed the drink, so her teeth, which are also mostly of calcium carbonate, would also have reacted, making her even more effervescent than she was reputed to be. I am sure too that a gummy Cleopatra would have been far less attractive to Antony, and nowhere do historians record that she subsequently wore false teeth. Now that is not to say that the incident did not take place, it is just that I do not think the pearl would have been dissolved in the assumed manner. Perhaps she just swallowed it with a gulp of wine, and the end result – an outrageously expensive meal, an early form of antacid, and an even greater hold over Antony – would have been the same.

Cleopatra's pearls would have almost certainly been from oysters living in the sea, but freshwater mussels also produce ones which are used in ornamentation. They have never been valued as highly as those from their seawater relatives, but in the days before pearls were cultured, they still supported a sizeable fishery in the colder lakes and rivers of Europe, including in Sweden. Living in that country in the mid seventeen hundreds was a scientist called Linnaeus, a man best remembered as the founder of the binomial system, the modern classification system of living organisms. He was the one who gave many animals and plants their scientific names, like mine, *Octopus vulgaris*. Not that there is anything vulgar about me, please note. The name *vulgaris* means common, in the frequently found sense of the word.

When not working out the natural relationships between various organisms, Linnaeus also discovered a way of culturing pearls in freshwater mussels. Several species of freshwater mussels can make pearls, but he used *Unio pictorum*, the so called 'painter's mussel'. He removed them from the water, drilled fine holes through their shells, and introduced tiny particles of limestone or plaster into their mantle. This would then have set off the reaction which produced the pearls, and to ensure they grew spherically, he supported them clear of the inner surface of the shell with silver wire. Having replaced them on the riverbed from which they had been taken, after six years, the pearls were fully formed. In 1762, Linnaeus sold his secret to a Swedish businessman, Peter Bagge, who was then granted a monopoly permit by the king of Sweden to develop pearl production. Strangely though, the technique was never exploited by Bagge, and Linnaeus' method was abandoned soon afterwards. It had to wait over one hundred and fifty years before William Saville-Kent came along and started to irritate the mantle of oysters.

Even freshwater pearl jewellery would have been too expensive for most people in Victorian England, but buttons made from mother-of-pearl were showy and affordable alternatives. Like all buttons, they had a way of becoming detached from the shirt fronts or blouse cuffs of their middle class wearers and dropping, unnoticed, to the ground. If that ground happened to be near a market stall, there was every possibility that the button would make a reappearance, but this time on the clothing of the costermonger who picked it up. Whereas originally the buttons had been functional as well as decorative, sewn onto the outer seams of the costermonger's garments, they now became purely for ornamentation.

These street market traders were almost as poor as the customers they served, and the times in which they lived were hard for the working classes. With no welfare system to support them, they relied on each other whenever they were ill or in need. Into this harsh world was born Henry Croft. Raised in an orphanage, he began work as a road sweeper in Somers Town market at the age of thirteen and quickly made friends with the costermongers. Inspired by their tradition of mutual support, Henry decided that he too should help the needy, including those living in his former orphanage. To do so he needed to raise money, and that, he believed, meant drawing attention to himself. Again he drew his inspiration from the costermongers and their pearly buttons. Over the weeks and months, he collected them and hand sewed them onto his cap. Then his jacket, his waistcoat and his trousers were covered, until he had created a whole suit of shimmering pearl, and he had become London's first Pearly King. I have a feeling that a suit covered in buttons made from wood or bone would not have started such a spectacular tradition. Today there are twenty eight Pearly families, one for each London borough, and each is headed by a Pearly King and Queen. Their costumes, thanks to the molluscs from whose shells the mother-of-pearl buttons were made, are just as elaborate as ever, and all maintain Henry Croft's philosophy of raising funds for charities.

9

'... of all the conchological cabinets in Europe...'

The National Museum of Natural History in Washington DC is home to 126 million items, making it the pre-eminent centre in the world for conservation, taxonomy and research in the vast field of natural and cultural science. With over eight million visitors annually, it is also one of the country's most important tourist destinations. Slightly more modestly, with a mere 80 million items in its collection, and a paltry half million visitors each year, the Natural History Museum in London also ranks highly in the league table of museums dedicated to the furtherance of understanding of the natural world. Their origins, however, were much humbler, and owe greatly to the unwitting contribution of millions of molluscs.

From as long as humans discovered there are places exist beyond their local horizon they have set out, by land or by sea, to explore them. Almost inevitably those lands were already inhabited by other humans, which gave them the incomers the opportunity to fight or to trade with the locals. In either event, when the explorers returned to their homeland they brought back with them tales of their exploits, and various trophies of their travels. Such souvenirs ranged from the gruesome, through the strange to the bizarre, and in most cases, the more unusual the better. A new species of bird or reptile might be interesting, but a furry animal with a beak like a duck and a tail like a beaver's, and given the name of a platypus, was far more crowd pulling. Coral that branched like a calcified plant, or resembled a brain, was a novelty seen in the natural state by just an adventurous few, whilst the elaborate headdress worn by the chief of a distant tribe spoke of the exotic way of life of its original owner. Some of the treasures brought back were fakes, such as mermaids made from the torso of a monkey skilfully sewn to the tail of a fish, or a horn of the fabled unicorn that transpired to be a tusk from a narwhal, but genuine or not, those with the means to do so gradually began to accumulate their own collections of curios. As both visually attractive and durable, shells were usually the most important artefacts, so the cabinets became a sort of molluscan mausoleum.

With few exceptions, collectors find a pleasure equal to the acquiring of their treasures in displaying and showing them to their friends, and one of the earliest people to have done so was the Neapolitan apothecary Ferrante Imperato. If, as the name of his cabinet of curiosities suggests, you have in mind a small display unit, rather like those used today for housing a collection of golf trophies, porcelain figurines or similar knick-knacks, then the term deceives you.

From medieval to renaissance times, a cabinet was a room in a private house – a kind of hybrid between a study and a man cave – and from an engraving made in 1599, Imperato's was just that. Four men are shown standing comfortably inside it, and every wall and even the ceiling has been made use of for storage and display. Even a full sized crocodile does not overwhelm the other exhibits with its size. Their arrangement, however, seems to be at random, with a scorpion adjacent to a starfish, and a hermit crab fixed beneath a grotesque animal with four legs, a wide flat tail, and a hideous beak. Taxonomically, it was as well organised as the tables in a village jumble sale, so would have had little value for scientific study. To do so, and as collectors made more and more additions, so they needed to become more systematic.

Ole Worm was one such person, and not being English was presumably not ridiculed about his name. He was a Danish physician who amassed a vast collection of fossils, minerals, weapons and costumes from native peoples, in addition to preserved animals, as evidenced in an engraving from 1654 of his cabinet of curiosities. Like Imperato's cabinet, many of his artefacts adorn its walls and ceiling, but on his shelves can be seen boxes clearly labelled as to their contents. *Animalium partes* is probably self-explanatory, as is *Metalia*, but his collection of molluscs is what particularly interested me. In a box of *Conchiliata* are large, spiny shells, quite recognisable as conchs, whilst near to it *Cochlea* contains more typical snail shells. Ole Worm had evidently appreciated the need to classify and catalogue if his collection was to have any value other than merely satisfying curiosity.

Sir Hans Sloane, now probably best remembered through Sloane Square and Sloane Street in London, was also a physician and an inveterate collector. Although born in Killyleagh in County Down, Ireland, when qualified, he set up his London medical practice in his home at 3 Bloomsbury Place. So successful was it that he numbered Kings George I and II, and Queen Anne as his patients. No doubt the fees he would have been able to charge them helped support his spare time passion. His interest in natural history stemmed from his Irish childhood, but blossomed when he became the personal physician to the Duke of Albemarle when he was appointed as Governor of Jamaica in 1687. Accompanying him to the island, he found himself surrounded by an abundance of new flora and fauna, so it was little wonder that on his return to England, he brought with him some 800 species of plants and animals. Not content with what he had managed to find for himself, Sloane was pleased to accept donations from friends and patients, as well as buying entire collections from other people. Unsurprisingly, his house became overcrowded with all he had accumulated, so to solve the problem he purchased 4 Bloomsbury Place, next door, to make more room. Even these two houses eventually proved insufficient, so in 1742 he moved his household and entire collection to his manor house in Chelsea. Collecting can be all consuming!

And a lucrative profession too. Born in 1791, Hugh Cuming grew up in West Alvington, a village in Devon, where he developed an early interest in natural history. No doubt the close proximity of the village to the Kingsbridge estuary was influential when it came to starting his collection of shells. In 1819 he left England for Chile from where, as a side-line, he was soon shipping plants and shells from South America back to his homeland. His exotic finds were eagerly purchased, often for very large sums, by those who wanted such rarities but were unable to find them for themselves. So profitable was this trade that in 1826 Cuming became a full time collector, and had a yacht specially built to accomplish his new work more effectively. Cruising the waters of the Philippines, around Singapore, St Helena, the Galapagos islands, and of the South Pacific, he dredged, picked up, bartered for and bought tens of thousands of specimens.

Through his discoveries and knowledge, Cuming became a well-respected authority on molluscs, and on his visits back to Europe he traded rare shells with other collectors. As Sir Richard Owen, the keeper of the Natural History museum in London wrote: *"It is this which has given him for some years past the command, so to speak, of all the conchological cabinets in Europe".*

Sir Hans Sloane and Hugh Cuming had more in common than being English conchologists; they were both anxious that, on their deaths, their collections should not be broken up, but made available to scientists in England. In his will, Sir Hans Sloane bequeathed his whole collection to King George II and the nation in return for £20,000 to be given to his heirs. Parliament debated this opportunity, and in June 1753 an Act established the British Museum, and Sloane's collection formed the basis from which it subsequently grew. In due course, Cuming's collection of shells was also offered to the by then established museum, which it purchased in 1866. It contained 19,000 species and over 60,000 specimens. In the words of Sir Richard Owen: *"...no public collection in Europe possesses one-half the number of species of shells that are now in the Cumingian collection".* At £6,000 it was a bargain at well below its market value.

Opened to the public in 1759, the British Museum's collections grew rapidly as, with the expansion of the British Empire, ever increasing numbers of artefacts were donated or purchased. Just as Sloane had needed more space, so too did the museum, and so the British Museum of Natural History was established in 1881 at its site in South Kensington. The curators also faced another problem encountered by Sloane and all other owners of cabinets of curiosity, that of preservation of their treasures. Fur, feather and skin were attacked by moths, beetles and microscopic agents of decay, while specimens submerged in alcohol or formaldehyde gradually lost their colours, but the calcified shells of molluscs remained largely unaffected by those ravages.

Today the British Museum holds a collection of nine million shells, many in as good a condition as when they were acquired, and as few major cities in the world do not have a museum of natural history, it is impossible to estimate the staggering number of mollusc shells there must be in their possession. Museums assert they are centres of conservation, yet within that term lies a great paradox. Those early avid collectors, with their cabinets of curiosities, laid down the museums' foundations, and they have indeed successfully conserved their specimens, but the very act of collecting has contributed to the extinction of species which can now only be seen as dead shells. The living molluscs are no more. As Donald Peattie wrote of Hugh Cuming in his 1938 book *Green laurels, the lives and achievements of the great naturalists: "On a reef in the South Seas (which has since been destroyed by a hurricane) he came on eight living shells of the "Glory-of-the-Sea". Almost fainting with delight he took all eight away, and it seems unlikely that the world will ever see any others".*

Fortunately Peattie was over-pessimistic, and the Glory-of-the-Sea (*Conus gloriamaris*) is still alive and well, but its story is illustrative of the threat so many of my fellow molluscs face. *Conus gloriamaris* is a cone shell with an attractive chestnut brown patterning, and specimens of up to sixteen centimetres in length have been found. It was first described in 1777, and throughout human history it has never been abundant, so consequently was particularly prized. After an auction in 1792 at which he bought one, it was recorded that a Danish collector (not Ole Worm) then destroyed it, thereby increasing the rarity value of his other one. True or not, by 1957 only about twenty specimens were known to exist, and could command prices in the region of $1,000 if sold. Since Cuming's discovery, no living ones had been found, but that changed in 1969 when more than one hundred were found alive by divers in the

Solomon Islands. Since then more have been reported, so the good news is that *Conus gloriamaris* is no longer under immediate threat of extinction, but sadly the same cannot be said for many other species of molluscs. In 2016, the International Union for Conservation of Nature listed eleven species of cone shells as endangered, and a further three as critically so. Even worse, 581 species of molluscs were critically endangered, with a further 507 on the endangered list.

That museums exist at all is in large part due to us molluscs, so those of us still alive hope that humans will learn a lesson from our exploitation over the centuries, and cease collecting all animals as curios, but content themselves with looking at them in their natural environment.

10

"Cursed before the Lord is the man who undertakes to rebuild this city..."

Whilst investigating a two thousand year old Egyptian mummy, the pathologist Armand Ruffer found tiny, calcified eggs of the parasitic trematode worm *Schistosoma heamatobium* in the kidneys. Trematode worms are a class of flatworms, so are much more closely related to tapeworms than to the earthworms with which most humans are more familiar. Ruffer's remarkable discovery added weight to the belief that the disease caused by this worm, schistosomiasis, or as it is more commonly known, bilharzia, was one from which the ancient Egyptians suffered. From their hieroglyphics, they were all too familiar with one of its symptoms, haematuria; blood in the urine. Its symbol was a dripping penis, and Ruffer's autopsy provided direct proof of its ancient occurrence, as well as founding the science of paleopathology. He recognised the eggs because some sixty years earlier, in 1851, another scientist called Theodor Bilharz first described the disease which bears his name. Bilharz had also been working in Egypt, at the Kasr-el-Aini hospital in Cairo, and made his discovery whilst carrying out a post-mortem on a much more recently deceased Egyptian.

The disease probably originated millennia before Ruffer's unnamed mummy contracted it, at a time when humans stopped being hunter-gatherers and became agriculturalists. Successful parasites need a stable relationship between themselves and their hosts, so when humans began planting their crops, and more importantly created large volumes of slow moving water for irrigating them, they inadvertently created ideal conditions for the disease to flourish. So even though it will never be known exactly how the unknown ancient Egyptian came to be infected, what is quite certain is that a mollusc played its part.

In defence of my fellow creatures, I should make it clear that the molluscs concerned, gastropod water snails called *Bulinus truncatus,* do not cause the disease. Indeed, they are as much victims as the humans; both involved in a continuous cycle of transmission. It therefore could be said, equally truthfully, that it is the humans which bring about infection of the snails. Perhaps before I go any further though, it would be worth explaining a little more about the disease itself.

The adult worm, or as human scientists prefer to call it, the fluke, lives in the blood, and depending on the species, within different blood vessels of the human body. Bilharz found his specimen in the hepatic portal vein, the vein which conveys blood from the intestines to the liver. Whichever the species though, their way of life is essentially the same. At about ten millimetres in length, the male is about half the size of the female, and tiny fertilised eggs are released by her into the blood. Producing many hundreds of eggs a day, she has a prodigious output. To continue the fluke's life cycle, these eggs much reach the outside of the body. Aided by spines on their surface, they first work their way through the walls of the victim's blood vessels and into the body cavity and then infect the surrounding organs. If these organs happen to be the bladder or the intestines, they will then be passed out with the urine or faeces, together with blood from the damaged blood vessels. Large numbers of these eggs in human tissues cause the other effects of infection such as inflammation, scarring, abscesses and pain on passing urine.

When the eggs hatch in water soon after leaving the human's body, they release a microscopically small swimming larva called a miracidium, and this is where the snail comes in. *Bulinus truncatus* only live in slow-moving water, and if the miracidium fails to find one, it will die, but if it does locate a new host it bores through its soft body and begins the next stage in the cycle. Inside the snail, and different species of fluke need different species of snails, the miracidium grows and develops into a new form called a sporocyst. Each sporocyst is capable of producing hundreds of further sporocysts, whilst each of these can make many larvae of yet another type, called cercaria. One miracidium can end up producing hundreds of thousands of cercaria, and each one of these is capable of infecting a human. Little wonder that the disease is so widespread!

The cercaria have forked tails and, once released from the water snail, they swim until they come across a human. Perhaps Ruffer's mummy at some time had been standing in the sluggish water of an irrigation canal along the banks of the Nile, when the cercaria would have bored through the skin. This would certainly have been the fate for some of the peasant farmers, and millions more like them in the centuries that followed, but the mummy was likely to have been of a much higher class. A more probable entry route would have been through the membranes of the mouth when the person took a drink of contaminated water. In any event, the larvae would have then entered the blood stream and matured into adult flukes.

It was not just the Egyptians who suffered from the disease. Ancient Assyrian records also note the bloody urine which it caused, and at about the same time that the person who was to become Ruffer's mummy became infected with schistosomiasis, Joshua was leading the Israelites across the river Jordan and attacking the city of Jericho. Jericho is one of the world's oldest towns and was probably in existence by 7,000 BC. An oasis in an arid land, its plentiful water supply makes it an ideal place for agriculture, and its name probably means 'city of palms'. A prize worth holding on to once taken.   Jericho's walls famously tumbled before Joshua's assault, but having captured the city he then cursed the place and left it uninhabited, saying:

> 'Cursed before the Lord is the man who undertakes to rebuild this city, Jericho. At the cost of his first-born son will he lay its foundations; at the cost of his youngest will he set up its gates.' (Joshua, 6:26).

According to biblical accounts, his curse held true, for many years later, Hiel of Bethel rebuilt the city, but he paid the prophesised price:

> 'He laid its foundations at the cost of his firstborn son Abiram, and he set up its gates at the cost of his youngest son, Segub,...' (1 Kings, 16:34).

When, later still, a group of Israelites had designs on living in the area, they reported back to Elisha that:

> '...this town is well situated, as you can see, but the water is bad and the land unproductive.' (2 Kings, 2:19).

Elisha remedied the situation by throwing salt into the spring from which the city's waters flowed. The biblical account of the abandonment of Jericho does not give an explanation of why this event took place, but we molluscs believe it was because of *Bulinus* and the trematode worms with which they were infected.

As an oasis city, water was the key to the city's existence. Cultivation would have depended on irrigation channels carrying water to the surrounding fields, and also providing an ideal habitat for water snails. With their thinner skins and employment in the fields, children would have been particularly vulnerable to infection by the cercaria released from them. Had Joshua actually realised the dangers of living in such an area and placed not so much a curse on the city as an early public health prohibition?

Humans might argue that my opinion is purely speculative, and I will admit there is no direct evidence that schistosomiasis caused Jericho to be abandoned. But we do know that the bricks from which the city was built were made of mud, and within these can be found large numbers of shells of water snails. From the archaeological evidence, we also know that one of these snails was *Bulinus truncatus,* the secondary host of *Schistosoma heamatobium.* To my mind the circumstantial evidence is compelling.

Jericho's subsequent re-emergence as a thriving city can also be attributed to us, but through our absence this time. Without any written molluscan records to draw from, I cannot be certain why it was that at the time of Elisha *Bulinus* disappeared from the region. It may have been through a changing climate which became unsuitable for them to continue to live there, or it may have been due to Elisha himself. Was the salt that he threw into the spring actually an incredibly effective molluscicide?

Today Elisha's spring still discharges clean water at a rate of 4,500 litres every minute, but this is too small for the city's population of nearly twenty thousand. Close by stands a modern pumping station that satisfies their demand without the risk of schistosomiasis. Or has it? With their ever growing populations, parched countries across Africa have turned to water storage schemes and irrigation projects, creating ideal habitats for *Bulinus* and schistosomiasis to prosper. There is not a man-made lake on the continent that is not a home to the parasite, bringing incalculable misery to the people who contract the disease. That engineering undertaking that was to control the Nile's flow, provide hydro-electric power for Egypt, and water for increased crop production, the Aswan High Dam, may have achieved those goals, but at an enormous cost to public health. It has been estimated that forty percent of the Egyptian population now harbour *Schistosoma heamatobium* in their bodies. Globally some two hundred million people in over seventy countries are ill with some form of the disease.

Through its molluscan secondary host, schistosomiasis was one of the tropical diseases which Europeans encountered as they started to lay claim to great swathes of Africa. By the end of the nineteenth century, no self-respecting European nation was without its "place in the sun". Cercaria larvae though did not discriminate about the colour of the skin that they penetrated, and white soldiers and settlers were soon falling victim to bilharzia. These unwelcome diseases began putting obstacles in the path of the ever expanding British Empire, so the British turned to medicine to overcome them. In 1899, the Liverpool School of Tropical Medicine was opened, followed shortly by its counterpart in London, and at the end of the century, one fifth of all British trained doctors were practising overseas. What a remarkable effect a snail, about ten millimetres long, had on an empire of four hundred million people.

Earlier, I did mention that there are other forms of schistosomiasis, and that transmission is also brought about by molluscs. So before I continue with *Bulinus truncatus* and *Schistosoma heamatobium,* I would like to say a little about two of them.

Oncomelania hupensis and other closely related snails inhabit slow moving fresh water in the Far East, where the irrigation channels serving paddy fields are ideal for them. It is their misfortune to be the secondary host to *Schistosoma japonica,* a species which infects water buffalo, sheep and goats as well as humans. *Schistosoma japonica*'s life cycle is broadly the same as that for *Schistosoma heamatobium* except that the adult fluke lives in the blood vessels of the intestines, so its eggs are passed out with their faeces. Faeces, both animal and human, have long been used to fertilise the paddy fields, so the cycle of infection was particularly hard to break, with miracidium larvae constantly attacking *Oncomelania* and, yes, cercaria larvae getting into humans. Nowhere more so than in China. Prior to the mid twentieth century at least ten million Chinese were infected, with whole villages left seriously under-populated as internal damage by the flukes led to early deaths of many of the inhabitants. With rice farming being such an important part of the economy, this must have had a profound effect on the country's development. Since then, control measures have improved the situation for humans, but I cannot help wondering whether China might have emerged earlier as a major power had it not been for the mollusc *Oncomelania*?

That other economic superpower, the United States of America, and where schistosomiasis does not exist, has also seen the cost of *Oncomelania* in both human and military terms. During the Second World War, United States' forces were engaged in fierce fighting with the Japanese, as they sought to liberate the Philippines and other Pacific islands. Battlefield casualties were high, and so too were instances of tropical diseases. More than three thousand soldiers were sent back to the United States suffering from schistosomiasis, at an estimated cost of three million dollars. Such financial figures may not have profoundly influenced the war effort, but put another way, it was the equivalent of putting three squadrons of P51 Mustang fighter bombers into action.

Quite probably, *Schistosoma mansoni* did not exist in South America and the islands of the Caribbean until it was brought there by humans. Unintentionally, of course, and almost certainly within the bloodstream of infected slaves being transported there from West Africa. As soon as the first eggs started to find themselves in water, so the larvae emerging into the New World would have sought out a new molluscan secondary host, and they found it in the form of several susceptible species of snails in the genus *Biomphalaria*. This was not their secondary host back in Africa, but it was one of those cases where a suitable alternative happened to be present.

From the mid sixteenth until the mid nineteenth century, about four million slaves arrived in Brazil to work on the sugar plantations. These were usually alongside rivers and streams, places which provided irrigation for the growing crops and from which drinking water was drawn for the workers, but also served as their sewers. All the conditions were right therefore for *Schistosoma mansoni* to take hold, and it certainly did. From a relatively few infected humans, the disease spread to the point that twenty five million Brazilians now live in parts of the country where it is endemic, and up to six million people are afflicted with it. There are those in the country who say that the European countries which were involved with the slave and sugar trades should now pay for the disease to be eradicated. Whilst this seems highly unlikely, if it did happen, it would almost certainly involve the elimination of *Biomphalaria glabrata* and other snails in the genus. From my perspective, this would be quite unfair since we molluscs were in Brazil long before *Schistosoma mansoni* arrived, so if anything should be taken out from the cycle of infection, it should be *Homo sapiens*.

So, after my little excursion out of Africa, let me return to that continent and to *Schistosoma heamatobium*. For the Europeans who first went exploring and then colonising the countries where it was found, its existence would have come as an unpleasant discovery. For European armies who invaded those countries it, together with a host of other tropical diseases, proved to be more deadly than the enemy.

When, in 1798, the French occupied the Nile delta, their physicians noticed the bloody urine passed by many of the Egyptian men. It was not long before their soldiers were doing the same. Ignorant of the cause, they put it down to the local climate and "faulty perspiration". Clearly serious precautions had to be taken to protect the soldiers' health, so they were instructed to wear condoms as a preventative measure! There appears to be no mention of how they were supposed to work, and whether Napoleon Bonaparte, the leader of the French army, wore one is not recorded either. What is known though is that in the years that followed his stay in Egypt, he suffered repeated bouts of dysuria, strangury and ischuria; afflictions as unpleasant as their names suggest. All result in painful urination and could well have been the consequence of *Schistosoma* infection.

Quite what makes large numbers of humans stand in a field and then proceed to slaughter each other, I will never understand. We molluscs do have some members which kill other molluscs, but never of the same species, and then only as a source of food. I am particularly partial to mussel and crab and, apart from the shells, I eat them all up. After a battle though, humans just dump the bodies of their dead in a hole in the ground and leave them to rot! From my understanding of *Homo sapiens*, it seems usually that the side which has lost fewest men declares itself the winner and attributes its victory to the brilliance of its leader.

With somewhere in the order of 46,000 men killed or wounded, on 18th June 1815, the battle of Waterloo was certainly a bloody affair. Slightly more French soldiers died than from the combined forces of the British and Prussians, and ever since then history books have recorded the outcome as a defeat for Napoleon Bonaparte. Certainly it was a decisive battle, precipitating an end to the First French Empire and the career of one of the world's foremost generals. What is in greater dispute is the reason behind his defeat. Human historians have variously attributed it to the stoic resistance of the British infantry squares against the French cavalry, to the timely arrival of General Blücher and the Prussians, and to the preceding days of rain which had softened the ground and made French advances difficult and tiring. We molluscs, however, have a theory of our own in that Napoleon's concentration was distracted by not being able to have a pain-free wee as a result of the schistosomiasis he contracted when he was in Egypt.

Following their victories, a grateful Britain erected monuments to its heroes of the Napoleonic wars. Wellington has his Arch near Green Park in London, his twenty eight feet tall Wellington Statue in Aldershot, as well as numerous others around the country, whilst Nelson stands proudly on his column in the middle of Trafalgar Square. How fitting it would be to have a monument to that unrecognised hero of Waterloo, *Bulinus truncatus* on its empty fourth plinth. Cast in bronze and even at ten times life-size it would be only as big as a Napoleonic cannon ball, so perfectly affordable in these austere times.

11

"You shall not accumulate the huo..."

In the summer of 1796 the Scottish explorer Mungo Park was deep in the interior of West Africa, destitute and starving. To make matters worse, he was the only European within hundreds of miles. Around him was unmapped land populated by wild animals and people of uncertain friendliness. That he was there was the result of having offered his services two years earlier to the African Association in Britain, which then appointed him to try to discover the source of the river Niger.

In June 1795 Park began following the course of the Gambia River inland for some distance and then struck off into the unknown. As an obvious outsider he should not have been surprised when a tribal chief took him captive and relieved him of his possessions. After four months Park succeeded in escaping with little more than his horse and the clothes he was wearing, but shortly after, through the kindness of the king of Bambarra, was given sufficient funds to help him continue his explorations. On 21st July 1796 he succeeded in reaching the Niger River, becoming the first European to do so. Running out of resources after a week of following its course downstream, Park was obliged to turn back, but still was able to chart its course for some three hundred miles. The third longest river in Africa had been fixed on the maps of Europe and a little more light shed on the 'Dark Continent'. And what form did the king of Bambara's gift take that made this possible? Although many miles distant from the sea, it was the accepted currency of the time in that region – cowrie shells.

Shells have been used as money by many peoples around the world, although cowries have been by far the most important in shaping the humans' world. Before I return to them though, I would like to take a little excursion to the United States of America.

In 1607, the British established their first settlement at Jamestown in the present day state of Virginia. Other colonies soon followed, the people eking out a living through growing crops, especially tobacco, for export back to the mother country, and by cutting down the dense forests for timber for Britain's naval and merchant fleets. Nobody appears to have given much thought for how all this was to be paid for and it was assumed that in return for their exports, the settlers would be supplied from Britain with the materials they needed. It soon became apparent that transatlantic supplies were not enough and the settlers needed to trade with the Native Americans too. It was here that they encountered a problem, for the gold and silver coins that the settlers had been familiar with in their homeland was not recognised by the Native Americans and so were worthless. Their currency was in the form of wampum, and if the settlers were to survive, they too would need to use wampum.

Wampum comes from the Narragansett Indian word 'Wampumpeage', meaning 'white beads strung'. These beads were made from mollusc shells; white ones from the North Atlantic Channeled Whelk, *Busycotypus canaliculatus,* and both white and purple from the quahog, *Mercenaria mercenaria.* The name quahog is itself also derived from the Narragansett word '*poquahock*', and when

Linnaeus gave the animal its scientific name, he judged that *Mercenaria* was appropriate. Derived from the Latin root for money, he was aware of its use as currency in seventeenth century New England.

To make the beads required time and a great deal of patience as a typical bead was only about ten millimetres long by five millimetres wide. Using a primitive drill, fine holes were made in pieces of the shells. Exerting too much pressure or trying to remove too much material at once would result in the shell shattering. Once finished, the beads were strung together and often worked into an ornate belt, for wampum was more than money for the Narragansett and other tribes of what became New England. It was an essential part of marriage ceremonies or as a badge of office, as well as a memory aid in the oral traditions of their customs and way of life, and might contain six thousand individual beads.

The quahog is an edible bivalve mollusc, an essential ingredient for a New England clambake and a favourite for making into clam chowder. They live buried in the muddy sands of estuaries from Canada's Atlantic coast to as far south as Texas. Each year they grow a little bigger, reaching a maximum size of about ten centimetres after about forty years. Some time before that, their shells are robust enough to be drilled, ground into the correct shape and polished for wampum. The dark purple quahog shells, being rarer, were naturally more valuable than the white forms.

The Channeled Whelk, *Busycotypus canaliculatus*, from which only white wampum beads could be fashioned, is a predatory gastropod often reaching ten centimetres or more in length and, like the quahog, is also eaten by humans. Rather than using the main part of its coiled shell though,

91

the Narragansett used only the columella, its solid inner spiral.

Whichever were used, the shells of these marine molluscs were also transported well inland, for the wampum belts were used not just by the coastal tribes, but by those far from the sea as well. Indeed, the land-locked Iroquois, living south of Lake Ontaria and to the west of the Hudson River, accumulated the greatest amount of wampum of any Native American tribe.

The newly arrived Europeans soon adjusted to using wampum as money, and from 1637 until 1661 it was legal tender in New England. Business with the native people increased, resulting amongst other things in a huge expansion of the fur trade, as Indian trappers exchanged animal pelts for wampum, but as with any currency, it was not long before unscrupulous minds got to work on exploiting it. Wampum was counterfeited. By staining white quahog shells dark their value could be doubled, so harsh penalties were introduced against the counterfeiters, and some colonies refused to accept dark shells at all.

For a currency to function it also needs to be fixed against other forms, and wampum was no exception. In British colonies a standardised six feet length of wampum had a recognised exchange rate with pounds, shillings and pence. A similar situation occurred in the Dutch colonies where it was set against their currency, the stuiver.

Alongside the expansion of the North American settlements, Britain's colonies in the West Indies were booming on the back of a burgeoning trade in sugar. Trade between these two outposts increased, but the West Indian merchants dealt only with metal coin. Gradually silver and gold became more acceptable to the Native Americans too, particularly as mass production techniques introduced from Europe devalued the wampum. In New England in 1661, wampum ceased to be legal tender, although it continued to be used in more remote parts of North America until into the nineteenth century.

From 1613 until 1664, the Dutch occupied a portion of the Atlantic seaboard which they called New Amsterdam. In that year it was captured by British forces and renamed as New York. As it had been for the British, the early days for the Dutch settlers were difficult times and trade, through wampum, had been essential for their survival. I feel it is fitting, therefore, that today's financial capital of the world, where 'money, money' is almost a mantra, should have been founded on *Mercenaria mercenaria*. And remember, the next time you hear someone telling you that they are going to have to 'shell out' to pay off their credit card bill that the expression hails back to that molluscan currency, wampum.

From that cold, Atlantic seaboard I will now head back to the warm waters of the Indian Ocean, home to the molluscs *Cypraea moneta* and *Cypraea annulus*. Known colloquially as money cowries, they are especially abundant around the Maldives Islands. These herbivorous gastropods are too small to be of any value as food, yet they became the world's first international currency. Collecting them in the earliest times was simple. Leaves from coconut palms were laid out in shallow water and the molluscs obligingly crawled onto them. The leaves were then pulled up, laid out on the beach, and the unfortunate snails left to die and dry in the sun.

In their own right cowry shells are beautiful; silky smooth to the touch and with the appearance of the finest glazed porcelain, so it is probable that their first use by humans was as jewellery. Perhaps one human saw another wearing one and hit on the idea of exchanging something of immediate worth, like food, for the pretty trinket of no intrinsic value. In turn that shell could have passed to a third person in a deal where the second owner received something that they needed. The step from bartering to the giving and receiving of money had been made.

Exactly when this happened, human history does not record. Chinese bronze objects from the thirteenth century BC suggest that shell money was in common use at that time, but it was not until the last century BC that there was written evidence. It was then that the Chinese historian S su-ma Ch'ien reported that cowries had been used as currency back in the Shang dynasty (16th-11th centuries BC).

We molluscs have only a limited understanding of modern human financial affairs. Suffice it to say that we know that the more money a person has, the greater their prestige appears to be and the more things they can buy with it. So if people have a surplus they tend to save it. And this was something they learned how to do from that early cowry money. During the Shang dynasty, the king P'an-keng reprimanded some of his ministers for hoarding cowries to the neglect of their duties. *"You shall not accumulate the huo...and make profits for your own use,"* he told them. 'Huo' was the word for money.

It was not only the Chinese who stored them up. In the late 17th century AD, the French navigator Pyrard de Laval was shipwrecked on the Maldives Islands and became aware of the export of cowries from there to India. He wrote that:
> *"The people of Bengal use them for ordinary money...; and what is more strange, kings and great*

lords have houses built expressly to store these shells and treat them as part of their treasure."

As a large transaction, such as building a house, could cost millions of cowries, their store houses must have been of quite a size themselves.

Fortunately for the continued survival of the money cowries, humans now use metal coins and paper notes as the basis of their currencies, but the shells foretold the properties that all coinage should have. Handiness was one factor. Typically *Cypraea moneta* is about twenty millimetres long, so they were small and easy to transport, and because they were all of a similar size, they could be weighed as well as counted. Modern bank tellers do much the same. Like coins too they were hard wearing, and just as they are readily recognisable, so were the cowries. So recognisable that they were very difficult to forge, and the cost of doing so was more than the value of the shell. Especially when inflation began to take its toll.

Humans often regard monetary inflation as a modern phenomenon, but it is certainly as old as shell money. To buy a woman in Uganda once required two cowry shells, but as more shells were imported into the country by Arab traders, so the price rose to as high as ten thousand. By the mid eighteen hundreds, the whole currency was being undermined. No longer was it worth counting shells individually but in fives and then piling them into heaps. For very large transactions they were put into sacks of twenty thousand! One of the causes of inflation was that traders began to use a related species of cowry, *Cypraea annulus*, which was found in huge numbers off the coast of Zanzibar. So great was their impact on the currency that the slaves who were used to carry these cowries from the coast of East Africa to inland Sudan began costing more in food on the journey than the value of the load they were carrying.

Cypraea moneta also demonstrated one of the fundamental laws of human economics, that of supply and demand. People today are familiar with the concept that the further away something is found from where it is produced, the more it is likely to cost them. They learned that from the cowries. On the Maldives many thousands would have been required to make even a modest purchase, whereas by the time they had been transported on arduous overland routes to China and Africa, their value had increased immensely. Arab traders visiting the islands could buy almost a million of them for one gold dinar, but by the time they had arrived in Nigeria, one gold dinar would get only one thousand for the new buyer.

Before I go any further, I would like to point out that *Cypraea moneta* did not choose to be used as currency. I say this because shell money could be used to buy anything in the countries in which it was used. On the west coast of Africa, traders exchanged them for spices, ivory and, highly significant in human history, for slaves. During the five centuries over which the slave trade existed, approximately twelve million people were transported across the Atlantic to work in the plantations of South America, the Caribbean and the southern states of America. At its height, the kingdom of Benin alone sold three thousand slaves a year. Quite how many cowries this would have involved is impossible to say, for in the early 1500s a typical slave bought there cost almost eight thousand shells. That amounts to about twenty four million in just one single year! If you then take into account that Benin was only one country involved, and that inflation would have steadily pushed up the numbers required to buy a slave, you can now understand why I cannot even guess at the number of *Cypraea* that would have been exchanged. Boatfuls certainly.

And that really was the case. Pyrard de Laval, during his two year stay on the Maldives islands wrote that cowries were exported:
> *"to all parts an infinite quantity, in such wise that in one year I have seen 30 or 40 whole ships loaded with them without other cargo."*

Through their use as money, the cowries therefore really did shape that terrible period in human history. By contrast though, they also helped lay the foundation of something which still flourishes today, the Chinese written language. You may be wondering how this could have happened, so let me take you back to the *huo*, the name given by the early Chinese for money.

Chinese writing is based on characters representing sounds or meanings, and back in the Shang dynasty, the character for money was PEI. This had developed from an earlier form of writing called the archaic script, where the symbol for money was a rough picture of the ventral surface of a cowry. Characters are, in turn, made of components called radicals, and PEI was adopted as one of them. Today, eighty four out of a total of the two hundred and fourteen Chinese characters have PEI as the main foundation. With a population of one point three billion and a literacy rate of ninety five percent, that means almost one and a quarter billion people in China look at characters based on *Cypraea*. Not bad for a small snail?

12

"May Ganges water and sea-chank betide..."

At some time between 8,000 and 2,500 years ago – humans can be irritatingly vague about dates sometimes – the Kurukshetra War took place. In what is now modern northern India, its outcome was destined to shape the history and culture of that country. A battle for the throne of Hastinapura in present Uttar Pradesh, between the armies of the Kauravas and the Pandavas - two groups of rival cousins and their allies - it was, as battles go, of truly epic proportions. Almost four million soldiers fought and slew each other until, after eighteen days, only twelve were left alive. With eight still standing on the Pandavas' side against only four on that of the Kauravas, the Pandavas were declared the winners.

Of those eight survivors, one was Krishna who was there in the earthly guise of the deity Vishnu. Having a god on the Pandavas' side must have given them a distinct advantage, and no less so when he was also their strategist. So, rather like in ancient European legends, the distinction between reality and fable is more than a little blurred, but the crucial role of the marine gastropod mollusc *Turbinella pyrum* in the Pandavas' victory is certain.

As was customary at that time, fighting took place only in daylight hours and was preceded by the blowing of conch trumpets which were fashioned from the shells of

Turbinella. Depending on how they are played, a range of tones can be produced, and the cacophony that was the prelude to the Kurukshetra War is recorded in the epic Indian poem, *'Mahabharata'*, when:

> *"... conchs and kettledrums, tabors and drums and cowhorns suddenly blowed forth with tumultuous clamour."*

No doubt such sounds were designed to raise the spirits of the soldiers, and just as drums and bugles were used to sound battlefield manoeuvres in the days before radio communications, so too were the conch trumpets. What a shambles the battle might have become had it not been for Krishna blowing on his conch to keep his troops in order.

Resembling enormous, thick-shelled whelks, *Turbinella pyrum* live in the Indian Ocean, where they can grow up to twenty centimetres in length. In life their shells are covered with a brown and velvety horny layer called the periostracum, which makes them inconspicuous as the animals plough through the muddy sands on which they live in search of worms to eat. Their death though transforms them.

On being fished from the ocean, the bulk of the body of the snail is removed and the almost empty shells stored in sheds sensibly located many hundreds of metres downwind from habitation. Over the next few days a multitude of maggots employ themselves in eating the remaining flesh, and as the outer layer disintegrates so it reveals the underlying shell which has the appearance of finest white porcelain.

Like whelks, *Turbinella* shells are spirally coiled and have a large opening through which the snail's foot emerges. To transform them into a trumpet, the apex of the empty shell is removed with a hammer and the aperture then polished smooth. From a strident blast akin to a huntsman's horn to the sonorous moan of a steamship's siren in a thick fog, each shell has a different voice and this can be further modified by altering the position of the player's lips when blowing.

Exactly how Krishna's conch sounded we will never know, but we do know that it had a name – Panchajanya. And in this he was not alone. Other Indian heroes had their named conchs:

> *"Panchajanya was blown by Krishna and Devadetta by Dhananjaya. Vrikodara of terrible deeds blew his mighty conch Paundra."*

As befitting the trumpet of a god, Panchajanya was no ordinary conch. Before Krishna took ownership of it, it had been the home of the sea demon of the same name and who inhabited the depths of the ocean. One day the demon made the fatal mistake of taking the son of Krishna's teacher captive and holding him to ransom, and when Krishna heard of this, he plunged into the water to rescue him. At the end of a monumental struggle, Krishna slew Panchajanya, brought away his conch shell as a trophy, discovered that it made an excellent trumpet, and named it after the dead demon.

The other feature that made Panchajanya different from most conch shells, and by a margin of about six million to one, was that it had an anticlockwise thread to its spire. *Turbinella* exists in two forms, with the overwhelming majority having a clockwise spiral or, to put it another way, when looked at with the tip of the spire pointing away and the shell's opening visible, the aperture is on the right. These are right handed, or dextral, shells, whereas Panchajanya was sinistral.

100

Without his conch trumpet to command the disposition of his troops, would victory in the Kurukshetra War have been Krishna's? Perhaps by way of answer, we should consider how he is usually depicted when he takes on the form of the god Vishnu. Notwithstanding that his skin is blue and he has four arms, he is essentially human in form. In each of his hands he holds a sacred object; a discus in one, a lotus flower in another, a mace in his third and a *Turbinella* shell, better known to Hindus as a sacred chank or shankha, in his fourth.

Vishnu, along with Brahma and Shiva, was one of the three gods responsible for creation. Before that there was silence, an emptiness called Shunyakasha, and as creation proceeded so the first sound was created. A deep, sonorous note, written as 'Om' or 'Aum', it is fundamental to Hindu beliefs and can be re-created by blowing into a conch trumpet.

From its mythical, and certainly military, origins, *Turbinella pyrum* became an essential part of Hindu spirituality. It was blown to call people to their sacrifices and other religious rites, invoked the attention of the gods before their ceremonies were performed, and helped prevent evil spirits from entering homes or temples. Due to their relative abundance, dextral shells are normally used for these purposes and are selected more for their tonal qualities than their size. No other instrument can produce the required sounds or maintain the reverential link with Vishnu.

If a temple is also fortunate enough to possess a rare sinistral form it will almost certainly not be used as a trumpet, but be exquisitely embellished with gold and silver and used as a libation vessel. Poured from such a shankha over the images of the gods, the water becomes holy as it leaves the shell. In his book *"The Indian Conch and its relation to Hindu life and religion"*, James Hornell quotes a Tamil proverb:

> *"If you pour water into a chank, it becomes holy water; if you pour it into a pot, it remains merely water".*

With changing times and the growth of secularisation, the importance of *Turbinella pyrum* in Hindu marriages may have declined, but just one hundred years ago it still had great significance. Hornell wrote that it had several important functions and reported that whilst no wedding bells pealed out in Bengal, instead the ceremony was accompanied by blasts on a conch and the recitation:

> *"May Ganges water and sea-chank betide*
> *Enduring bliss to bridegroom and bride."*

To help ensure that 'enduring bliss', the marriage was not legal unless the bride had chank bangles placed on her wrists, and even today many Hindu brides are still given them at their wedding.

India is the second most populous country in the world and has a population of over 1.2 billion. Of those, eighty percent consider themselves to be Hindu. That equates to 960 million people in India alone whose beliefs and culture have been directly shaped by the mollusc *Turbinella pyrum*. Without wishing to blow its own trumpet, that is quite an achievement.

13

"...I stole the idea of his house..."

A mollusc shell is one of the few products of nature which look almost as beautiful after the original inhabitant has died as it did when it was alive. With some shells the colours retain their vibrancy long after death, but with the exception of the most fragile, their form degenerates only gradually with the passage of time. Such qualities are probably what makes them so fascinating to humans, and there can be few who have not picked one up and admired it. Young humans seem especially attracted to them, and will spend happy hours on a beach collecting them, perhaps to take home as a way of remembering their visit, or to use them to decorate their sand castles. So perhaps it was a re-kindling of childhood memories that inspired Francisco del Rio Cuenca to go one step further and adorn his house with them.

Francisco lived many miles from the sea in Montoro, near Cordoba, in southern Spain, so it is unlikely that as he was constructing his new house he was envisaging such a project, but that is where chance played its part. Close by to where he was working in 1957, a lorry dumped thousands of scallop shells, and Francisco seemed to have been a person not to pass over an opportunity. During the course of the next three years, he carried hundreds of bags of the shells from where they had been left back to his house, initially with no clear idea of what he was going to do with them. By the time the building work was over though, he had decided to embed them into the rendering with which he was coating the outside. This would, he believed, save the need to re-paint every year, and give it a more individual appearance.

Standing between houses whitewashed in the traditional style of the region, Francisco's house was certainly eye-catching, with its outline, as well as every door and window, picked out in a swirling mosaic of shells. As word of his creation spread, so visitors came to view it, many of them bringing more shells with which he could continue his enterprise. Mussels, top-shells, murex, ormers and carpet-shells soon increased his palate of shells with which to work, and inspired by what he had achieved, he set about encrusting the interior walls, the stairs, and even the ceilings, until he had covered every possible surface. Eventually, many millions of shells became incorporated into his designs, and the house has become a tourist attraction in the region.

I can easily understand Francisco's motivation, for we octopuses also like to personalise the crevices in which we live. Biologists have long noted the presence of small stones, pieces of broken glass, bottle tops and, of course empty shells, around the entrance to our lairs, and suggested that we do this as a way of camouflaging it. Nonsense! Just as they like to hang a basket of flowers by their front door, or stand tubs of them on their doorstep, so we also like to make our home more inviting. Rather disparagingly, some of them refer to these areas as middens, but I resent the connotations the term implies, preferring to call my little patch a garden. Don't you think calling it an octopus's garden sounds much more entrancing? Ringo Starr certainly did.

In the summer of 1968, whilst working on their *White Album*, tensions between the members of The Beatles reached a point where Ringo temporarily walked out of the famous Abbey Road studios. By way of a break, he took his family on holiday to the Mediterranean where the comedian Peter Sellers had lent him his yacht. Off the coast of Sardinia, he and the yacht's captain began talking about octopuses, apparently as a consequence of Ringo being served with squid rather than fish, and during that conversation Ringo was told about the octopus's curious habit. As he later wrote: *"I thought this was fabulous, because at the time I just wanted to be under the sea too."*

Ringo set about writing the lyrics and the music, and in early 1969, he and George Harrison began to work it into the song with the title of *Octopus's Garden*. It was only the second song that Ringo had written, and may well have been judged by the musical colossi that were John Lennon and Paul McCartney to have been inferior to their own work. *Octopus's Garden* was considered for inclusion in the *Let It Be* album, but it was not until work began on the *Abbey Road* album that it was finally recorded, being released in September of that year.

Abbey Road was an outstanding success, with four million copies being sold in the United Kingdom in the first two months after its release, whilst in the United States it remained the top selling album for twelve weeks. Many critics consider it to be the Beatles greatest compilation, and it consistently appears highly placed in polls which rank 'best ever' albums. It must also have one of the most recognisable covers of all time, with the four Beatles striding across the zebra crossing outside of the Abbey Road studios. Thousands of Beatles fans have subsequently crossed in joyful imitation, as others have done so in parody, making it a major tourist attraction. To protect it, in 2010, the crossing itself was given grade II listed status.

Even I would hesitate to say that Abbey Road's success stemmed solely from Ringo Starr's song, and in turn the octopus's gardens which inspired it, but as one of the ten tracks on the album, my molluscan relatives do deserve some credit.

Francisco del Rio Cuenca was not alone in covering his house with seashells, and there are examples to be found all around the world, although most do tend to be at the seaside. Like Francisco's house, they attract and entertain the curious, but none have the visitor numbers and artistic influence of Postman Cheval's Ideal Palace.

Ferdinand Cheval lived in Hauterives, a village in southern France a short distance to the north east of Valance. In April 1897, at the age of forty three, he was returning from his postal round when he came across an unusually shaped stone. It proved to be the stimulus for him single-handedly building a palace unique in the world; an undertaking that consumed his every spare moment for the next thirty three years, amounting to a staggering total of ninety three thousand hours.

At first glance the Ideal Palace looks like it has been transplanted from Angkor Wat or some other eastern temple, with ornate pillars, towers and buttresses reaching up to ten metres in height, but all cultures and religions, the sacred and the secular, are to be found here; Cheval's fertile imagination set in cement. As he wrote: "*The fairies of the East come to fraternize with the West*".

At a length of twenty-six metres and with four facades, the building follows no architectural rules. A Swiss chalet sits next to an Arab mosque, a larger than life sized Caesar, Archimedes and Vercingetorix stand shoulder to shoulder, and snakes and alligators slither past a Phoenix and the Minotaur. So complex, so grand, yet with such fine detail, it is impossible to state to which movement of art Cheval's masterpiece belongs. Some see elements of Baroque in it, others claim it is Naïve, yet most agree it is the work of a self-taught genius.

Cheval began his massive undertaking by firstly clearing the vegetable garden behind his house, and for the next two years created his fountain "The Source of Life". Encouraged by the favourable comments of his family, he then continued extending what is now known as the East façade, even incorporating into it a tomb in which he hoped to be buried. In due course, the other four facades were built, until in 1912, he finished.

All of Ferdinand Cheval's creations were made of stones he gathered as he delivered the post around the district, and which he then set in lime, mortar and cement. To further embellish them, he also incorporated seashells, sent to him by a relative living in Marseilles. Whelks and winkles, clams and cockles, scallops, tellins, and an abundance of oysters, all feature as integral parts of his handiwork.

It had been his intention to be buried in a tomb within his Ideal Palace, but for reasons of public health, this wish was refused. Undeterred, and at the age of seventy seven, Cheval then set about building his own tomb in the nearby village cemetery. Although more modest in scale, it is every bit as elaborate as his Palace, and the use of shells even more marked. In Ferdinand Cheval's words: *"Many visitors will also visit it after seeing my "Palace of Dreams" and return to their country in amazement, telling their friends that this is not a fairy tale, but true reality."*

Not everyone was as encouraging as was his family, and during his lifetime many in the village mocked and criticised him. Nevertheless visitors did come to see his handiwork, even as it was in progress, and gradually his fame increased. Sadly the extent of his genius was not recognised by other artists until after his death. The founder of Surrealism, André Breton, visited the Palace several times during the 1920s, and pointed out Ferdinand Cheval as the precursor of Surrealist architecture. Picasso visited him in 1937, and tributes to him have been paid by Max Ernst, Jacques Brunius, Niki de Saint Phalle, and Jean Tinguely amongst many others. In 1969, the then Minister of Culture, André Malraux, himself an art theorist, had the Ideal Palace declared to be an historical monument.

From using shells to decorate a building, it requires only a small step in the human imagination, although a much larger one in the engineering, to construct one in the shape of a shell. Of course, mollusc shells are the ideal home for the molluscs that inhabit them, so a degree of ingenuity is needed to make a shell-shaped building functional.

Situated off the Yucatan peninsula of Mexico, the Isla Mujeres is bathed in the warm, clear waters of the Caribbean Sea, and due to its proximity to several coral reefs, it has become a popular tourist destination. When the architect Eduardo Ocampo bought a plot of land with sea views there in 1994, he built two houses, one for himself, and the other for his brother Octavio. At various times, Octavio has been a film actor and director, a dancer, and a sculptor, but he is best known as a prolific surrealist painter. It seemed fitting, therefore, that the house that Eduardo designed for Octavio should resemble the sea shells that were so abundant around the island.

The house, which took three years to complete, is constructed in two parts, a single storey made to look like a top-shell, attached to one of two-storeys in the form of an enormous conch. There are doors where the operculum of both snails would be, but realism can be taken only so far, so Eduardo installed windows in what would otherwise have been the solid shell. Nothing is angular, and even the doors and windows have curved profiles. The molluscan theme is continued inside, with a spiral staircase giving access to round rooms with shell-crusted bookcases, and ornamental vases themselves in the shape of shells. Even the shower head in the bathroom is made from a spindle shell.

Painted a dazzling white, the house is certainly eye-catching, but I am still far from certain in my opinion of it. If imitation is the sincerest form of flattery, then I feel I should be pleased that an architect has transformed our houses into a human living space, but part of me says that the house is simply kitsch. As a holiday home it is a quirky novelty, fun almost certainly, but would anyone want to live in it permanently?

The Guggenheim museum in New York though, that is an altogether different matter. Frank Lloyd Wright, its architect, used nature as his muse, but did not attempt to copy it. Advice given by him to his students was to *"Study nature, love nature, stay close to nature. It will never fail you."* Having created one of the world's most iconic buildings, he seems to have been correct.

Frank Lloyd Wright began his design in 1943 and devoted sixteen years to the enterprise. It was also to be one of his last, for, at the age of ninety two, he died six months before it opened in October 1959. During that time, his grandson, Eric Lloyd Wright, was an apprentice working on the project, and he remembered that: *"...every Sunday at breakfast he'd give us a talk... And sometimes he would have placed before him a whole bunch of seashells. And he said, "Look here, fellows. This is what nature produces. These shells all are based on the same basic principles, but all of them are different, and they're all created as a function of the interior use of that shell."*

Indeed it was a shell on which he based his design, transforming the raw materials of concrete and steel into a cylindrical building that is wider at the top than at its base. Reflecting its outward appearance, internally it has a spiral ramp which rises from the ground level to just beneath the skylight. It was this slanting spiral ramp which initially brought criticism from artists who questioned whether paintings could be displayed properly on it. Lloyd Wright faced down his critics and his design went ahead.

When he undertook the Guggenheim commission, the spiral design was not a totally new concept in Lloyd Wright's mind. In 1925 he had worked on the grandly named Gordon Strong Automobile Objective and Planetarium. Rather like a modern multi-storey car park, here motorists would drive upwards on an external spiral ramp and leave their car with a valet at the top. Whilst the valet then returned the car to the ground level, the motorists would descend on a pedestrian spiral, admiring the surrounding countryside before then entering the planetarium. Gordon Strong was unhappy with the plans, and the project never came to fruition, but the creativity behind it is clear. As the architect wrote to him: *"I have found it hard to look a snail in the face since I stole the idea of his house—from his back."*

And which snail might it have been in the case of the Guggenheim museum? I have seen it written that the design was based on the shell of the Nautilus, and whilst this is not unreasonable as its shell is indeed a spiral, it is, however, essentially a flat one. Contrast that with what I believe is a far stronger contender, the Japanese Wonder Shell (*Thatcheria mirabilis*). Here the helical spiral is truly three-dimensional and resembles an auger that could be used for drilling into the ground. Place an image of the museum and one of the shell next to each other, and the similarity is immediately obvious.

So unusual is its shape that when a specimen was first brought to England in 1897 by Charles Thatcher, some conchologists believed it was a fake. Any doubts about it being a real mollusc, albeit a rather rare one, were subsequently dispelled when further specimens were obtained. Little is known about their ecology other than they live in deep water in the Pacific Ocean, and even their relationship with other gastropod families is uncertain.

In one respect, whichever shell served as the model for Frank Lloyd Wright's creativity is irrelevant. The important point is that the Guggenheim museum remains a cultural icon of avant-garde architecture thanks to a mollusc.

14

Spain 1, Netherlands 0

The Nobel Prize for Physiology or Medicine for 1963 was awarded to John Eccles, Alan Hodgkin and Andrew Huxley. It was in recognition of their work on '*ionic mechanisms involved in the communication or inhibition of impulses across neurone membranes*'. To put it in more straightforward language, they had solved the problem of how nerve impulses work. A neurone is a nerve cell, and the message it carries is called a nerve impulse. Because the impulses often have to be carried over considerable distances within the body, neurones are typically extremely long and fine, a bit like telephone wires. These long extensions are called axons.

To carry out their investigations the scientists wanted to put one electrode inside an isolated nerve cell axon and another one on the outside of its membrane. They would then stimulate the axon electrically and, using an oscilloscope, measure and record changes in the charge across the membrane as the nerve impulse passed between the electrodes. It is this change of charge that sweeps along the axon membrane of the cell which actually is the nerve impulse. A major problem confronting them though was that human nerve axons are only about one micrometre – that is about one one thousandth of a millimetre - in diameter; far too tiny for even the finest electrodes to fit inside. Fortunately for the researchers, the diameter of nerve cell axons of invertebrates is often considerably larger. Some are so large that they are referred to as giant axons, with a diameter of up to one millimetre.

Much of the research by the Nobel Prize winners was carried out in the laboratories of the Marine Biological Association in Plymouth, and it helped open up the field of neuroscience and human understanding of diseases of the nervous system. The location was also perfect for other important key participants in the experiments, namely the Atlantic Squids whose giant nerve axons were used in the investigations. So vital was the part they played, it seems extremely churlish of the Nobel Prize committee not to grant them also the recognition that they deserved.

The Atlantic Squid, or *Loligo pealei*, in common with all its relations in the class Cephalopoda, use giant axons as a means of sending stimuli to muscles faster than along their normal nerve cells. As a rough rule, the greater the diameter, the faster the speed at which the impulse travels. Fast muscle reactions are important particularly in escape reactions when the squid might be attacked by a predator. If this happens, the muscles surrounding the mantle cavity contract violently, forcing the water already within the cavity, together with some ink, out through a narrow opening called the siphon. Long before Sir Isaac Newton set down his Third Law of Motion, which states that: *"when two objects interact, the forces they exert on each other are equal and opposite and are called action and reaction forces"*, *Loligo* was well aware of the consequences.

The jet of water gains momentum in one direction whilst the squid gains it in the opposite one. Or to put it another way, the squid shoots off rapidly, leaving its bemused attacker staring at an inky cloud and wondering where it has gone.

Attaining speeds of up to twenty five miles per hour, this jet propulsion makes *Loligo* the fastest of all marine invertebrates. Not as fast as the jet aircraft or rockets made by humans, granted, but using a propulsion system which works on the same principles. And the use of swivel jets for short take off aircraft was also worked out by *Loligo* millennia before humans even existed. Their siphon, on the underside of their body, can be angled to enable them to jet off in almost any direction.

Now I cannot prove that *Loligo* had a direct influence on the thinking of Sir Frank Whittle, Werner von Braun or any other human involved with jet or rocket engine development, but it would be nice to think so. I can say, however, that the other trick used by *Loligo* and many of its relatives in evading their enemies, ink, did have a direct influence on human society.

Squids, octopus and cuttlefish, all cephalopod molluscs, produce ink when attacked. They store it in ink sacs near to their gills and release it with the water from their siphon so, temporarily hidden behind the screen of pigment, the animal can then make good its escape. Unless the attacker happened to be a human and they were caught. Their most likely fate would then have to be eaten, but some would have been used as a source of ink, and each type of cephalopod produces a slightly different coloured pigment. That of the octopus is black, squids produce blue-black, whilst that from cuttlefish is a reddish brown and known as sepia.

Humans have been using inks for writing since they gave up scratching marks into clay tablets and wanted a pigment that could be applied to papyrus, parchment or paper. Oxides of metal ores, carbon, and plant extracts have all been used throughout the ages, and no one knows who the first people were that hit upon using ink from squids and their relatives. It's a fairly safe guess to suppose they lived by the Mediterranean Sea though, and the Greeks and Romans certainly used it. Indeed the Latinised, scientific name for the European cuttlefish is *Sepia officinalis*, which in turn is the Latinised form of the Greek word for cuttlefish, σηπία, *sēpía,* and from which the name of the ink itself is derived.

To make the ink, the ink sacs were removed from the unfortunate animals and dried in the sun to prevent them decaying. Once dry, they were dissolved in dilute alkali and the resulting liquid filtered to extract the pigment. The pigment was then precipitated and neutralised using hydrochloric acid, washed, filtered and dried. To improve adhesion, gum arabic or shellac might also be added to act as a binder. It was then ready for use by the writers and artists of the ancient world.

Would the works of Aristotle, Homer, Pliny and Tacitus have survived and still be read by humans today if the ink with which their words were recorded had faded to illegibility? And what of the sepia sketches and studies that artists have made over the centuries?

Leonardo da Vinci certainly used it, and his stature as one of the world's most famous artists might well have been less had it not been for *Sepia officinalis*. Leonardo was a true Renaissance man who took a keen interest in the natural and man-made world around him, as testified by the wealth of material within his sketchbooks. Whether it was his design for a fiendish new war machine like his *'Battle Cart with Mobile Scythes'*, or a *'View and Plan of a central space church'*, a study of *'The Proportions of the Human Figure'* or of *'Five Grotesque Heads'*, many were drawn in pen and ink.

If not the *'Portrait of Lisa del Giocondo (Mona Lisa)'*, then Leonardo's most celebrated work must be *'The Last Supper'*. Painted in oil and tempera on plaster in the refectory of the Monastery Santa Maria delle Grazie in Milan, it changed the way that the theme was portrayed, with Judas now placed behind the table at which Jesus and his disciples were seated, rather than in front. It is a work which has been extensively copied and parodied since the late fifteenth century when it was created, and helped propel him from being a court artist to Ludovico il Moro in Milan to one accepting commissions from wealthy patrons across Europe. The creation of Leonardo's masterpiece was not though just a matter of drawing on the refectory wall and then colouring in the scene. Rather it was the result of the genius of his painstaking preliminary studies. The attitude of the head of Saint James the Greater in a study from 1495 is almost identical with that in the finished work, whilst the vitality of the scene is vividly captured in his *'First Sketch for the Last Supper'* drawn in the same year. And the medium in which they were worked? Brown ink, of course.

While the cuttlefish who gave their lives in the production of sepia ink may take posthumous comfort from being immortalised in works of art, those alive today are more likely to be relieved that pigment technology has moved on. Synthetic inks, paints and dyes have now replaced natural ones, although the warm brown tones produced are still referred to as 'sepia'.

Photographers also have adopted the name. In the early days of photography, the black and white pictures they printed so commonly faded under the influence of light to shades similar to sepia drawings that people began to assume that they had been made that way. In turn monochrome was superseded by colour film, with ever better colour rendition, but tradition dies hard. At the click of a computer mouse button, a modern digital colour image can be transformed into an arty or nostalgic sepia photograph.

The ancient Greeks did not just owe us molluscs a debt of gratitude for their two dimensional work in writing and drawing. They have to thank us for inspiring their architecture as well. From those times right up to the present day, humans have admired the graceful symmetry of Classical buildings, with their triangular pediments supported by elegant columns, and of the various styles of columns, perhaps the most iconic is the Ionic.

An Ionic column is characterised by the volutes of its capital, soft, gracefully swirling scrolls cut into the solid stone. The style originated in Ionia, the south western coastland and islands of present day Turkey, and one of the earliest examples can be found in that country in the Temple of Artemis at Ephesus. Ancient writers regarded the temple as one of the Seven Wonders of the World. Would it have been so viewed without its striking Ionic columns?

History does not record which Ionian mason first cut the now so familiar design into the stone. It is possible that he was also a mathematician, for the shape is a special type of spiral curve called a logarithmic spiral. It follows an exact sequence as you measure from its centre outwards and its form has fascinated thinkers such as Descartes and Jacob Bernoulli through the centuries. It was Bernoulli who gave it the name 'the marvellous spiral' or *Spira mirabilis*. What a misnomer. He should have called it *Spira nautilus*, for it is my belief that the Ionian stonemason was not following a mathematical formula, but copying the shape of a shell he had found washed up on a beach. The curve of its shell too, when cut in half, is a logarithmic spiral.

The genus Nautilus, which contains *Nautilus pompilius* and five other genera, is the last vestige of a once prolific subclass of molluscs called the Nautilodea. Now endangered, their ancestors first appeared some five hundred million years ago and were roaming the world's oceans long before the era of dinosaurs. Today they are restricted to the warm waters of the South Pacific. As swimming molluscs they are relatively slow movers compared with squids and cuttlefish, and spend the day quietly in deeper water. At night they move into shallower parts, seeking out their food of dead or dying invertebrates through their sense of smell. In turn, they gain protection from predators through their calcareous shell.

A fully grown *Nautilus* is about the size of a human hand's span, with the shell forming an upward flat spiral - a bit like a Phrygian cap with more curls - and the animal's head and arms emerging from the open end. The inside of the shell is lined with mother-of-pearl, and is sub-divided into as many as thirty chambers. As the animal grows, so it creates a new chamber into which it moves, leaving the older ones empty and sealing them up. It is these gas filled chambers which produce a natural buoyancy and which could have helped keep an empty shell afloat as it drifted with the ocean currents into the Mediterranean Sea and architectural immortality.

The temples of ancient Greece would have been places to which people went to pray to their gods and ask the soothsayers for predictions about their future. Would they be healthy, would victory be theirs in battle and would wealth be coming their way? Modern day humans have much the same questions in their minds, and when the football World Cup of 2010 came along millions of people were eager to hear what fate might have in store for their team. Pundits voiced their opinions, team form was studied, bookmakers laid down their odds, and from his aquarium in Germany, Paul the Octopus became an international celebrity.

Paul's correct name is *Octopus vulgaris*, with the *vulgaris* meaning common and certainly not vulgar. Not that there was anything common about Paul. Quite the contrary. In 2010 he was already famous for having correctly predicted the outcome of four out of six of the German football team's games in the 2008 EUFA Cup. The world, and particularly the Germans, waited to learn how he thought they would fare against countries not just from Europe this time, but from around the world.

That Germany would beat Australia in their opening fixture was Paul's first prediction, and few would have doubted his opinion. He was to be proved correct, but that he felt Germany would lose to Serbia in the next game of the group stages sent waves of disbelief around the country. Surely he had got it wrong? No, he was quite correct and fortunately for the Germans, despite their defeat, they still qualified to move into the knockout stages.

It was his prediction that Argentina would lose to Germany that got Paul into hot water with the Argentines, and it would have literally been true if Argentine chef Nicolas Bedorrou had been able to get his hands on him. He posted a recipe for octopus on Facebook when Argentina lost and Paul was correct again, proving that an octopus can be much more than calamari.

Germany was now looking on course for a place in the semi-finals against Spain. It must have been a tough decision for Paul to have made when he chose Spain to win, for the calls for him to be eaten, when he was yet again correct, were then being voiced in his own homeland. Leading Spanish politicians offered him protection, but security at Paul's aquarium was tight and he lived to give the waiting world his ultimate prediction; who would be the winning finalists? In maintaining his one hundred percent success rate, Paul had opted for Spain over the Netherlands. They won, by one goal to nil, but hardly had the sound of the final whistle died away though when some people were being critical of him.

To indicate the team he believed would win a game in the competition, Paul was required to choose a piece of his favourite food, some fresh mussel, from one of two containers. Each container was marked with a flag, one for Germany and the other with that of the opposing country. For the final, one bore the Spanish flag and the other that of the Netherlands. For all the matches, the first piece of food picked by Paul was his way of showing which team he favoured to win. Nothing special there, a fifty-fifty chance, his critics carped. No better than throwing a coin. Possibly, but over eight games, the probability of getting all the outcomes correct was $1/2^8$ or 0.39%. In betting parlance that is 256 to 1; odds that most people would rarely go for if they were backing a horse. How many football pundits did as well? To riposte, those same pundits might well reply that they did not just say which team they thought would win, but also what the score was likely to be, and that was something which Paul never did. My answer to his detractors is that no one bothered to ask Paul.

15

"O death, where is thy sting?"

I Corinthians 15:55

In June 1935, Charles Garbutt was on a pleasure cruise off the Queensland coast of Australia when he put ashore on Hayman Island. He was a fit and healthy twenty seven years old, and in training for football. As he strolled along the beach, so he came across a seashell about the size of a lemon, and covered with a yellowish skin giving it a rough appearance. Perhaps he could see that beneath that layer was a much more colourful shell; creamy white overlain with brown or red mottled patterns. Gripping it in the palm of one hand, so the open side of the shell was in contact with his skin, he then proceeded to scrape away at the rough layer, called the periostracum, with a knife. Almost immediately he began to experience a slight numbness in his hand, whilst after ten minutes his lips were beginning to feel stiff. By twenty minutes his sight was blurred and he was seeing double, and after another ten minutes his legs had become paralysed. He was obviously seriously ill, and by the time he reached a doctor, he was in a coma. Five hours after handling the shell, Charles Garbutt was dead. Reported in *The Medical Journal of Australia* during the following year, his case is one of the few confirmed fatalities as a result of being stung by a cone snail, although non-fatal incidents are much more common.

Cone snails are marine gastropods inhabiting tropical and subtropical seas, from the inter-tidal zone to deeper water, and living buried in sand or on rocks and coral reefs. All belong to the genus *Conus*, which contains over six hundred species, so it is little wonder they can be found in such a wide range of habitats, yet they all have in common that they are predatory carnivores. They are also slow moving so instead of running down their prey, they use a venomous harpoon made from a modified radula tooth. In most gastropods, the radula resembles a miniature file covered with tiny, hard teeth, and which it uses for scraping its food into its mouth. You can sometimes see the marks left by a grazing pond snail if you look at the inside of the glass of a neglected fish tank. In the case of a cone shell though, the teeth are hollow, barbed, and filled with venom. When a prey animal ventures near, the snail pushes out its long, flexible, tube-like proboscis, and through it fires a radula tooth, with almost instantaneous results. As the radula tooth is still attached to the radula itself, the snail then retracts it and pulls the paralysed prey into its mouth.

The cone snail's prey are as varied as their habitats, and are usually marine worms, other molluscs and even small fish, but as Charles Garbutt discovered to his cost, they will also use their poisoned radula to defend themselves when being attacked. I feel sure that his attempt to scrape off its periostracum would have greatly annoyed the animal he was holding, so my advice to would-be shell hunters is to look but not to touch. Cone snails' venom can also be far more deadly than might be imagined to be required to subdue their prey. Mr Garbutt was unfortunate in having picked up a specimen of the Geography Cone, *Conus geographus*, one sting from which is estimated to contain sufficient toxin to kill at least fifteen people. Looked at in another way, a lethal dose to humans is as little as 0.005 milligrams per kilogram of body weight. This makes it one of the world's most deadly animals. Even today there is no known anti-toxin, so treatment of someone who has been stung is simply to try to keep them alive until the effects eventually wear off.

Charles Garbutt succumbed to an appropriately named conotoxin, which is a cocktail of short chained neurotoxic polypeptides. Put more simply these are small proteins which affect the nervous system. We came across the idea of the transmission of a nerve impulse back in chapter eleven, so I would like to take our understanding of it just a little further. Bear with me, it is important.

Nerve impulses work by chemicals such as sodium and potassium entering or leaving the nerve cells themselves, and they do so through sub-microscopic holes in the cell membrane called channels. Impulses may also trigger a muscle to contract, and again, its contraction is due to a movement of the same chemicals. If the chemicals cannot move, the nerve impulses do not work, and the muscles will not contract. Scientists are now beginning to understand how some of the conotoxins work; that is by them stopping the flow of the chemicals through the channels. Charles Garbutt's symptoms can now be explained as the nerves and muscles that kept him conscious and breathing progressively stopped functioning.

The exact composition of a conotoxin varies from one species of Cone snail to another, but scientists have isolated some and have found they have very specific actions. For example, δ-conotoxin stops sodium channels functioning, whilst α-conotoxin blocks the transmission of an impulse from a nerve cell onto a muscle cell. These findings have enormous significance for humans in the potential treatment of memory loss, epilepsy, and drug and alcohol withdrawal symptoms, as all of these involve the transmission of nerve impulses. So too does the perception of pain, and here humans need to be really grateful to *Conus geographus* as one of the conotoxins isolated from its venom, and known as Con-G is a powerful analgesic. Known commercially as Ziconotide, it is much more effective than morphine in controlling pain, and with the additional benefits that smaller doses are required, it has less side effects, is non-addictive, and patients are less likely to develop tolerance to it. Perhaps some good came from Charles Garbutt's fatal encounter after all.

Competing hard with Cone snails for the title of the world's most venomous animal is another marine mollusc, the Blue-ringed octopus, or more accurately the several species of the genus *Hapalochlaena*. They inhabit rock pools and coral reefs of the Indian and Pacific Oceans, where they feed on crabs, shrimps and other crustaceans, and for most of their time they remain invisible, concealed within crevices. When threatened with danger however, they warn their potential predator of their poisonous potential by becoming a highly conspicuous bright yellow in colour, accentuated by a large number of iridescent, flashing, bright blue rings.

Not infrequently, Blue-ringed octopuses appear on the sea shore or in shallow water where they attract the attention of the curious beach walker. Being relatively small in size, with a maximum arm span of about twenty centimetres, they almost invite being picked up. In October 1954, off East Point Beach near Darwin in Australia, the companion of a twenty one year old man named Kirke Dyson-Holland did just that. He then gave the octopus to Kirke, who placed it on his shoulder for a short time, before tossing it back into the sea. At that point his companion saw a small trickle of blood coming from where the octopus had rested, and shortly afterwards Kirke began to experience difficulty in breathing. As his condition deteriorated, so he was taken to hospital where on the way he was heard to say: *"It was the little octopus"*. By the time he arrived at the hospital he was not breathing, and his heart stopped some fifteen minutes later. It was estimated the time between him being bitten and his death was one and a half hours. Although the octopus which bit Kirke was thrown back into the sea, his companion subsequently found one which he said was identical, and this was identified as the Southern Blue-ringed Octopus (*Hapalochlaena maculosa*).

As with other cephalopods, an octopus has a horny beak with which to bite into its prey, and in the case of the Blue-ringed octopus toxic saliva is then poured into the wound. The toxin has been identified as tetrodotoxin or TXX, a poison so deadly that twenty five grams – about the weight of four stock cubes – is sufficient to kill ten men. Like that from Cone snails, there is no antidote, and somewhat like conotoxin, that of the Blue-ringed octopus also inhibits nerve impulses by blocking sodium channels. Once again, if the nerves cannot stimulate the muscles required for breathing to work, respiratory failure and consequent lack of oxygen to the brain will bring about death.

At the time of writing, I am unaware of any research being undertaken to use this knowledge in the production of a pharmaceutical drug, but no doubt it will be only a matter of time before it is.

Partly through their eye-catching colouration, Cone snails and Blue-ringed octopuses have inflicted harm, but also brought potential health benefits to humans. They are also relatively unusual creatures, so few people will have encountered them at first hand. The same is much less likely to be said about the Blue mussel (Mytilus edulis), a familiar, though dull, sight on the inter-tidal zone of shores

125

around the world, in the fishmonger's tray, or served up on a plate as moules frites. Like all bivalves molluscs, they are filter feeders, straining the water that passes over their gills for microscopic food, but unlike the majority of their two-shelled brethren, they do not live safely buried in sand or mud, but instead choose to live on rocks often exposed to the full force of the waves. They arrive on the rocks as larvae drifting in the plankton, but once in contact with a solid surface, they immediately begin to secrete strong threads which glues them in place. These byssal are similar to those produced by *Pinna nobilis* in chapter four, and are, of course, waterproof.

This ability to set under water inspired researchers to find out what made this possible, and they came up with the answer – dihydroxyphenylalanine. This is an amino acid (a building block of all proteins) found in large concentrations in a family of proteins called, somewhat prosaically although accurately, mussel adhesive proteins. A group of biomedical engineers at Northwestern's McCormick School of Engineering and Applied Science then began applying this knowledge in a ground-breaking technique which they published in the *American Journal of Obstetrics and Gynecology*.

During pregnancy it is possible for the membrane around the developing baby to become punctured. If this occurs, the amniotic fluid in which the baby is bathed will leak out, resulting in premature birth or a natural termination. Sometimes a self-repairing mechanism operates, but if it does not, there is no current way in which the hole can be sealed. Using in-vitro techniques, the McCormick team, together with colleagues from other countries, put small holes in the amniotic membrane, and then used a variety of materials to try to repair them. Success was judged according to the best ability to bond and toxicity to the membrane's cells. Of all the materials tested, the sealant based on mussel adhesive proteins was the most effective. The next steps will be to see how strong the seal proves to be, and to carry out in-vivo experiments in animals.

For a mussel to stick itself onto a rock is one thing, staying there is another, so the byssal threads have not only to be well glued on, but not break when the animal is heaved about by the waves. Researchers Zhao Qin and Markus Buehler have come up with the way in which they do it, and published their findings in their snappily titled paper, *Impact tolerance in mussel thread networks by heterogeneous material distribution.*

It was already known that byssus is very flexible yet also exceedingly strong, so what they discovered was that it was made of a soft and stretchy material at one end, and of more rigid material at the other. About eighty percent of the strand is composed of the stiffer material, with the more stretchy component making up the other twenty, which the researchers likened to a bungee cord. The researchers are now thinking how this ratio could be used in creating a similar synthetic material. With the properties of strength and elasticity, they say it would be ideal for surgical sutures after heart and stomach surgery, where irregular movements place a great strain on them. Such material would also be ideal for repairing or replacing human tendons. Tendons, of course, connect bones to muscles so, and - please excuse the play on words, but how could I resist it? – that must be very gratifying for mussels.

16

Crying cockles and mussels

Through the pages of this book, I have shown how molluscs have influenced the culture, society, history and economics of humans, but there is still no escaping the fact we are also nutritionally very important to them. When Molly Malone wheeled her famous barrow through the streets of Dublin, she was plying a trade which had sustained humans for millennia; a trade which is at least equally important today. As a fishmonger, it is almost certain that she would have had a diet rich in seafood, and although the health benefits of such a diet were not scientifically recognised until quite recent times, she should have been able to look forward to a long and healthy life as a consequence. What a bitter irony it was, therefore, that she died of a fever before she reached old age.

It is of course possible that the fever she contracted, like that of the sixty three fellow guests who dined at Winchester with the unfortunate Dr William Stephens, came from her own shellfish. Perhaps she would have been wise to have followed the public health advice given in Leviticus 11, verse 10: *'But all creatures in the seas or streams that do not have fins or scales – whether among all the swarming things or among all the other living creatures in the water – you are to detest.'* Nothing then was known about the link between water-borne diseases and contamination from human sewage, but the circumstantial evidence must have been clear enough to Moses.

Today, with that understanding clear, provided that we have been reared in uncontaminated water, we are perfectly safe to eat, and humans are continually extolling our virtues. We are an excellent source of protein, and globally molluscs contribute about three percent of protein intake. Whilst this may not seem a particularly high figure, the distribution of consumption is far from uniform. Seafood provides more than 3.1 billion people with almost 20 percent of their average per capita intake of animal proteins.

Beyond being simply a source of protein, over many years health campaigns have also sought to promote the other benefits to human health brought about through eating seafood. When you look at some of the figures for what molluscs can do for you, it is hardly surprising.

Take clams as just one example. A three ounce serving (about eighty five grams) will give an average adult human more than its entire daily requirement of vitamin B_{12}. This vitamin is essential for the protection of nerve cells and supporting the transmission of nerve impulses, so it is little wonder that eating shellfish is thought to help protect against memory loss and dementia. That same serving will also provide more than the daily requirement of iron, essential for red blood cell formation and the efficient transport of oxygen around the body. Its deficiency causes anaemia which, according to the World Health Organisation, affects half of pregnant women in developing countries, and accounts for twenty per cent of maternal deaths.

Cardio-vascular disease affects at least twenty five percent of the human population, yet eating seafood once or twice a week is likely to reduce the risk by as much as thirty percent, with the greatest benefit being for older women. A high intake of seafood has also been associated with a decreased risk of ovarian and colorectal cancer. Similarly, in post-menopausal women, the incidences of breast cancer appear to be lower in those who eat seafood as their main source of protein in preference to red meat.

Older humans may well gain a disproportionate benefit from seafood. Age-related macular degeneration is a relatively common disorder of the eye in the elderly, and results in a progressive loss of vision. A number of studies indicate the value of one or two seafood meals a week in protecting against this condition. As a rich source of vitamin D and calcium, which are both required for maintaining healthy bone structure, the elderly are also likely to suffer less from osteoporosis.

Globally, the production of fish, crustaceans, molluscs and other aquatic organisms continues to rise. According to figures from the Food and Agriculture Organisation (FAO) of the United Nations, in 2014 it reached 167.2 million tonnes. Of this, 93.4 million tonnes were captured, and the remainder reared through aquaculture. Molluscs contributed one quarter of the total, and of this, almost two thirds was derived from aquaculture.

By far the greatest amount of molluscs consumed are marine species, with less than five percent coming from freshwater. Clams, scallops, oysters, and mussels are all important, but of those marine species, I find it upsetting to discover that, at more than sixty percent of the total, catches of squid, cuttlefish and octopuses top the table and far outweigh any other group. In terms of value, molluscs are worth over thirty three billion US dollars annually, so considering our disproportionate sacrifice, I also find it rather galling that us Cephalopods constitute only one third of the molluscan total. Clearly humans do not value us that highly.

The scale and importance of fisheries across the world is almost impossible to overestimate. There are in excess of four and a half million vessels in the world's fishing fleet, with three quarters of them being in Asia, and over fifty six million people are directly employed in the industry. Fish accounts for seventeen percent of the global population's intake of animal protein, although the relative importance between different countries is marked.

Seafood consumption in the United Kingdom is an excellent barometer of the state of the nation's economy. During the Second World War, when fish was one of the few sources of protein that was not rationed, consumption was as high as it has ever been, but as post-war prosperity increased, and cheaper meats became more widely available, so demand dropped by about fifty percent. It remained at much that same level until the country was hit by the recession of the mid-1970s, when it fell by another one third. As the country gradually recovered sales started to rise again, and continued to do so until the recession of 2007 struck, when once again demand dropped dramatically.

Currently the annual consumption of seafood is in the region of four hundred and eighty nine thousand tonnes, but a breakdown of that figure reveals much about the eating habits of British humans. Fresh salmon tops the list of what they eat, accounting for about fifteen percent, whilst fish fingers, at about seven percent, are slightly more popular than haddock. From a molluscan point of view, I am delighted that the British do not seem that keen on us. Mussels constitute only one percent of their seafood intake, whilst squid, cuttlefish and octopuses comes in at a mere nought point four. You might even say that the British public prefer just about any other seafood much more than calamari!

Printed in Poland
by Amazon Fulfillment
Poland Sp. z o.o., Wrocław

58505818R00078